The Mystical Filmmaker

The Mystical Filmmaker

An Encounter

24 July 2009 – 19 August 2010

Peter Whitehead
John Sorensen

Sticking Place Books
New York

www.stickingplacebooks.com
www.onceoutofnature.com

Design by Ryan Bojanovic
(cover after a design by John and Mary Condon)
www.bojanovic.com

ISBN 978-0-9905308-5-5

In his suggestive and allusive language, the mystical filmmaker often approaches the methods of music. When he does this, his statements do not give information. They operate a kind of enchantment which dilates the consciousness of the audience to a point at which it is able to apprehend new aspects of the world.

– after Evelyn Underhill

Fragments

This book is offered as a complement/addendum to the primary works of Peter Whitehead, which are his films and fiction. It shows another aspect of Whitehead's persona: the way he interacts in dialogue – in the give-and-take of ideas; in the frisky and fierce tango-ballet of spontaneous written word-play. It exposes his marvelous gift for finding myriad connections between a host of subjects that are "in play" in a living conversation.

There are plenty of good Whitehead monologues available, but it's nice to hear him in duet, as well; to see him in a pas-de-deux. Many filmmakers are interesting in an interview setting, where they can tell stories and be the raconteur – but there are very few who would be so engaging in the context of an epistolary-dialogue.

There is a dramatic unity to this correspondence. It's not "just a bunch of letters" written over a rambling period of time – it is, rather, a complete and concise conversation-in-writing, with a distinct beginning, middle and end: a conversation that took place almost entirely within the time-nutshell of six-months. It's a conversation that would never have happened if not for the completion of Peter's *Terrorism Considered* film and the terrible coincidence of the sudden death of his daughter.

At its best, I feel that the correspondence has a vibration not unlike Antonin Artaud's description of Balinese theater, and it reminds me of Artaud's declaration that actors "should be like torture victims who are being burned and making signs from the stake." Because of the painful context of these letters, I feel that, sometimes at least, *The Mystical Filmmaker* is a collection of "signs from the stake."

John Sorensen
February 2014

Pierrot & you
Friday, July 24, 2009 1:52 PM
From: "john sorensen"
To: peter whitehead

Dear Mr. Whitehead,

My friend Paul Cronin has kindly shared your e-mail address with me and I am now using it to bother you with a question or two.

I admire your many works: on film, in print and elsewhere – perhaps in conversation (via Paul's films) most of all. In the past few weeks, I've felt a great debt of gratitude to you for the wonderful job you did in preparing the published screenplay of 'Pierrot le fou.' I watched the newish Criterion version of the film recently, and was overwhelmed by the experience. Immediately I wanted to enter more deeply into the film, and I found a grand passageway through your transcription. Your notes and descriptions helped me in so many ways to know the story better and to live in it longer.

At the same time, new questions arise for me, and I wonder if you might help me with a few of them. The first, and most curious, is a choice that you made in translating a key line in the film. The line occurs in the scene [p. 57 of your book] with Marianne and Ferdinand 'curled up on the beach.' They discuss the man in the moon for a spell. At the end of their exchange, Marianne seems to say to Ferdinand: 'Baise-moi.' The Criterion version translates this line as 'Fuck me.' Your version, however, has 'Stop it, stop it...' I wonder why you translated the line as you did. Am I – and the Criterion folk – missing something here?

In a more general sense, I'm curious to know your process in making this transcription. I assume it was done from the French release print. Is this correct? Any recollections you have of the process (did you discuss it with Godard at all?) would be most welcome. I wonder, as well, what are your thoughts about this 40-year-old transcript/screenplay. Were you pleased with the results – or are there afterthoughts/concerns/regrets that have come into play since that time – things that you wish you had or had not done?

Finally, as it is clear that Godard has been an important figure in your own creative life, I wonder how – after all these years – you feel about his work in general, and about films such as 'Pierrot le fou' in particular... and how you feel about your own creative connection to him/them today.

I'm a bother, I'm sure – but hope that I'm not too much of a bother.

In any case, I thank you for being Peter Whitehead, and I hope to hear from you soon.

Peace,
John Sorensen

Re: Pierrot & you
Friday, July 24, 2009 3:53 PM
From: "Peter Whitehead"
To: john sorensen

Dear John

I am busy putting the final touches to my new film. I am sure Paul can give you a copy of the recent edit – work in progress. I give permission. But it means I can't at present answer at length. Sorry.

I worked on Alphaville without a script and did all translations direct from a print. With Pierrot I had a dialogue script to translate. I presume the UK distributors who lent it to me had the "Fuck" altered. I didn't notice. Quite an alteration.

DVD

Monday, February 1, 2010, 5:33 PM
From: Paul Cronin
To: "sorensen"

John I have a DVD for you of Peter's new film
Sad news though: one of his daughters died last week...

pjc

shanti shanti shanti

Wednesday, February 3, 2010 9:59 PM
From: "john sorensen"
To: "Peter Whitehead"

Dear Peter,

I've just watched your new film, which Paul Cronin kindly gave to me this evening. Your dear labyrinth of images and words and music and sounds has touched me deeply and unexpectedly. I sat down at the dvd machine only to determine whether or not the disc would play properly in it (an earlier copy wouldn't run) and thinking that, perhaps, I'd watch two or three minutes just for a preview. As it happened, I didn't move from before the screen for two hours and thirty four minutes and forty four seconds – at the end of which I was tired but very happy. I don't quite know what I think. Perhaps I don't think anything at all. But certainly I am happy. Thank you for this beautiful thing.

shanti shanti shanti

j

p.s. Paul has told me of the sudden and terrible loss of your daughter, and I am filled with sorrow and concern for her, for you and for all of your dear ones. You are in my prayers and peace-wishes. If there is anything I may do to be of help in this difficult time, I am here and ready.

Peace,
John

Re: peter's film
Thursday, February 4, 2010 9:43 AM
From: "Paul Cronin"
To: "john sorensen"

John,

I received an email from Peter. He wrote of receiving an email from someone with SHANTI SHANTI SHANTI at the start. Was that you? He accidentally deleted it. If this is you, please re-send your email. He very much wants to read it. Peter says he is living in Hell.

pjc

your beautiful film (again & still)
Monday, February 15, 2010 11:25 AM
From: "john sorensen"
To: "Peter Whitehead"

Dear Peter,

I continue to meditate on your beautiful new film, which holds a special fascination for me. There are elements at play in it that I find particularly intriguing and elusive – many of which have to do with the Feminine Spirit that engulfs the entire work: specifically the sense of the Feminine as creator and destroyer. The very term 'eco-terrorist' suggests this duality, I think. The multitude of Marias makes me think not only of the Virgin but also of the Goddess Kali. (Perhaps the 'shanti shanti shanti' at the end of the work summons up the Hindu connections in me, I don't know.)

I spoke with Paul concerning some of these thoughts and, in the course of our talk, quite a number of other fascinations began to form in my mind: the connection of Michael Schlieman and that other Schlieman(n), who went in search of Troy and, inevitably, Helen (another example of 'fatal beauty')... I wonder: is there a Maria Leblanche as well as a Maria Lenoir? I don't know.

Perhaps my thoughts are just silliness, but I enjoy them all the same. Most especially as related to that scene near the end with Schlieman and the Maria played by the quite extraordinary Sophie Strohmeier. In the cat and mousing of that fairly-ultimate conversation, I couldn't help feeling that

Strohmeier's Maria was the very Maria that she would see "soon" – perhaps later today or tonight. Certainly by tomorrow.

A week or so before watching 'Terrorism Considered' I happened to view Godard's 'Hail Mary,' and the experience of his Maria is also somehow bound up with my experience of your many Marias.

As well, I feel that the long flow of messages displayed on the screen throughout your film is the only truly joyful experience of 'texting' that I've yet had in the age of the twittering machine.

I hope these thoughts are not incomprehensible or unwelcome, and I wish you all good things, now and ever. Your film helps me in ways that I can't explain – an experience which is quite alright with me.

Peace,
John

Re: your emails
From: Peter Whitehead
To: Paul Cronin
Date: 23 February 2010 22:27

Dear Paul

Please tell John I was very touched by his amazing email to me – which is why I have been silent since. I want to do him justice. Not had the peace of mind to write as I would like to. His comments on my film were 1000% accurate. Devastatingly so.

peter.

Re: your beautiful film (again & still)
Sunday, February 28, 2010 5:00 PM
From: "Peter Whitehead"
To: "john sorensen"

Dear John

Your email moved me to tears! Sorry for delay in replying. I have been burying my daughter... the most precious person to me in all the world.

I am indeed the broken man – of the film – now. I now see the whole film as the final fall inside the city of Vienna – which is my body... dying from the inability in such a domain to truly access the feminine... yes the film is about my myth. The search for wholeness with, through and inside the labyrinth which is the Feminine... body and soul.

I used the Shantih quote because it is the last line of T S Eliot's The Waste Land. He once said he should have been a Buddhist – but decided it was fake to assume he could be while living in the West. So of course he grappled with the mysticism of the High Church of England. Producing The Four Quartets – which I rate as highly as Rilke's Elegies – they float in the same whirlpools...

Yes I chose Schlieman from the start of my writings. He is the de Quincey figure (or Wilkie Collins maybe)... who digs into the deceiving grassland... to find the lost buried city (Jung) in search of The Lost Girl... soul... anima. Helen in MS's case...

JS: 'Is there a Maria Leblanche as well as a Maria Lenoir? I don't know.'

PW: In the film there is a voice when MS dies... saying "Where are you?" This is REAL! A voice of one great love of mine... La Blanche... BIANCA...

Jagger of course. So, yes, Maria le/la Blanche... is there. I would say there is a hint in Sophie's comments at the end... talking of entanglement. I see Lenoir (NUT – LEILA... KALI) entangled with the light, as is the thunder entangled with the lightning... Mark Twain and Tesla. (Google them together! you will see they were referred to like this...)

JS: 'Most especially as related to that scene near the end with Schlieman and the Maria played by the quite extraordinary Sophie Strohmeier. In the cat and mousing of that fairly-ultimate conversation, I couldn't help feeling that Strohmeier's Maria was the very Maria that she would see "soon" – perhaps later today or tonight. Certainly by tomorrow.'

PW: Yes... perhaps her own dead self. Or she would return to being her true self... who IS Maria Lenoir...

JS: 'A week or so before watching 'Terrorism Considered' I happened to view Godard's 'Hail Mary,' and the experience of his Maria is also somehow bound up with my experience of your many Marias.'

PW: I especially watched Godard's Hail Maria during the making of this film – and the editing. I was going to use some quotes but finally didn't. Too obvious. A very very important film – as is the accompanying film by his "Maria"!

JS: 'As well, I feel that the long flow of messages displayed on the screen throughout your film is the only truly joyful experience of 'texting' that I've yet had in the age of the twittering machine.'

PW: Yes I was pleased with them. A Professor in Vienna said they were an embodiment of Derrida's ideas... re... the postcards.

Send me your address. I will send you a couple of my novels.

JS: ‘I hope these thoughts are not incomprehensible or unwelcome.’

PW: neither... I am very happy to send postcards... and receive them! (post-modem-cards?)

very best wishes to you

shantih shanti shanti

pre & post cards
Sunday, February 28, 2010 6:42 PM
From: "john sorensen"
To: "Peter Whitehead"

dear peter,

thank you. your message has touched me as deeply as your film. maybe they're both parts of the same good and difficult gesture – which is, for many reasons, a much-needed thing in my life at this moment.

your film and message, coming at this time, is a true comfort (remembering the root of that misused word: to 'comfort' another person is to 'share strength with them' [fort = fortitude]). you may be a broken man, but still you help to heal the wounds of another. i'm grateful.

you and your daughter are very much in my thoughts and prayers, every day. i feel the devastation of this loss: in your letter and in your film, too. i really can't separate the experiences now.

one reason that your work resonates so powerfully in me is that your myth is a myth that lives in my own life. as you perfectly express it: 'The search for wholeness with, through and inside the labyrinth which is the Feminine... body and soul.' i think this phrase may be written somewhere on my birth-certificate.

here are a few of my thoughts on your thoughts on my thoughts:

– I used the Shantih quote because it is the last line of T S Eliot's The Waste Land...

– do you know the version of the upanishads that was co-translated by w.b. yeats? in this lovely book, yeats and swami shree purohit translate 'om shanti shanti shanti' as 'may peace and peace and peace be everywhere.' your words remind me of this, and of the fascinating introductions that evelyn underhill wrote to the memoir of rabindranath tagore's father ('autobiography of debendranath tagore') and to the translations of kabir's songs, which she made with r. tagore. in her writing/work of this period (c. 1914), underhill often uses an intriguing phrase: 'the completing opposites,' which has become very important to me.

– Yes I chose Schlieman from the start of my writings. He is the de Quincey figure (or Wilkie Collins maybe)... who digs into the deceiving grassland... to find the lost buried city (Jung) in search of The Lost Girl... soul... anima. Helen in MS's case...

– forgive me if i free-associate (i'm in that kind of mood), your lines reminded me of this segment from... i don't remember where... but referring to a passage in the 'devi bhagavatam purana,' in which:

"The creator god Brahma tells the story of how he, with other male deities, once visited the Goddess. At first, they were not sure whether She was one of the holy Nymphs: so beautiful She was, seated on Her cot, in red clothes, jeweled and radiant-faced. As the gods approached Her, they were themselves turned into beautiful women, and they realized that She was surrounded by millions of other women – all forms and manifestations of Herself. As She smiled at them affectionately, the deities suddenly saw in

Her pink toe-nails a vision of the entire Universe, with its continual waves of movement and change, its cosmoses, oceans and mountains. They stayed there for a hundred years, welcomed by all the attendant women and happily enchanted by their charms."

Vishnu, who was one of the gods, composed a hymn in honor of the Goddess, in which he praises Her as the great cause of all manifestation, change and dissolution – for the whole Universe rises out of Her, rests upon Her and melts away into Her. From Her are crystallized the original elements and qualities which construct the apparent world. And what is more, the gods themselves are merely constructs out of Her maternal substance, which is both consciousness and potential Joy. One passage of Vishnu's hymn is specially enlightening:

"Now I realize that only You are the ancient eternal Prakriti (Nature, or Form-and-change). From staying with You, I see that it is You who mercifully teach the knowledge of the Brahman to the ancient Purusha... and only thus can he realize his eternal nature. Otherwise, he will always remain under the delusion that he is the Lord, the Purusha without beginning, the good and universal soul, and so fall into all the [ruinous] forms of egoism... It is You, Mother, who have put out from Yourself the representations of all the visible worlds for the Spiritual benefit of living creatures, playing all the parts in the theatrical play."

– In the film there is a voice when MS dies... saying "Where are you?" This is REAL! A voice of one great love of mine... La Blanche... BIANCA... Jagger

of course. So, yes, Maria le/la Blanche... is there. I would say there is a hint in Sophie's comments at the end... talking of entanglement. I see Lenoir (NUT – LEILA... KALI) entangled with the light, as is the thunder entangled with the lightning... Mark Twain and Tesla. (Google them together! you will see they were referred to like this...)

– thank you telling me of the voice. i will listen for her when i next see/hear your film. thanks, also, for the tesla/twain connection, this is a new discovery for me. i am in love with this quote from tesla:

"I had hardly completed my course at the Real Gymnasium when I was prostrated with a dangerous illness or rather, a score of them, and my condition became so desperate that I was given up by physicians. During this period I was permitted to read constantly, obtaining books from the Public Library which had been neglected and entrusted to me for classification of the works and preparation of the catalogues. One day I was handed a few volumes of new literature unlike anything I had ever read before and so captivating as to make me utterly forget my hopeless state. They were the earlier works of Mark Twain and to them might have been due the miraculous recovery which followed. Twenty-five years later, when I met Mr. Clemens and we formed a friendship between us, I told him of the experience and was amazed to see that great man of laughter burst into tears."

– Send me your address. I will send you a couple of my novels.

– thank you for this kindness. i won't be in nyc for the next few weeks, so please wait to send any mailings until near the end of that time (if they arrive before 23 march, the post office may send them back to you, since i won't be here to pick them up).

thank you for all.

may peace and peace and peace be everywhere,

j

film
Tuesday, April 6, 2010 7:53 PM
From: "Peter Whitehead"
To: "john sorensen"

John

The film was interrupted half way through. After only 3 months of working on it – with The Bambis film group.

I got very very very ill – a serious attack of Reiters Syndrome Auto-immune disease.

It meant I abandoned the film and Vienna – had to come back to survive – because it could easily destroy my heart – down to 41% extrusion factor. Stress is not good news. I was ill for nine months with it. Agony.

I was living at the time with Samantha Berger – one of the most fascinating girls I have ever met – and loved! She moved out of my flat when I was lost back in England.

When I got back to Vienna I found that I had lost Samantha – with whom I had done most of the filming – I was told she had had a breakdown and disappeared. Probably gone back to PERU. And I had also lost NINA of the Bambis. So I had no film essentially. I had lost Maria and Yoko!

But then I had met Sophie before – got in touch again and found out that she was working in the Third Man Museum. Asked her to be in it. And she was perfect.

When I was 95% through editing the film – a month from completing it for the Viennale... I discovered that Samantha had killed herself less than a month after I had left for England.

She had seen me in the worst state of the attack. She went to the highest building in Vienna and threw herself off.

And now Robin is dead... also.

It has not been an easy journey

best wishes
peter w.

your difficult myth
Tuesday, April 6, 2010 10:35 PM
From: "john sorensen"
To: "Peter Whitehead"

Dear Peter,

I am, at present, about halfway through my reading of the book-version of 'Terrorism Considered...' which speaks to me as a kind of coded-confession: in a language that I'm certain I'll never be able to deeply comprehend. And (perhaps since I don't mind not knowing things) I'm enjoying it very much. It's fascinating to observe the dance of connection/disconnection between the word and the image versions of your difficult myth, and I grow ever more curious to return to the film to 'see what it says' to me in the aftermath of my reading.

As well, Paul has kindly shared with me a collection of your film works, which I've been exploring in-between-times. I deeply respect your gifts as a filmmaker, but sometimes I come away from my viewings with the sense that – as good a filmmaker as you certainly are – you are an even better cluemaker.

In watching 'Nothing to Do with Me,' I became curious to know if you have ever taken an interest in the writings of Martin Buber (especially 'I and Thou'). Buber's I-Thou/I-It ideas seem very connected to some of your thoughts in that intriguing short film – and beyond.

Could you please tell me more about the notebooks you kept during the filming of 'Terrorism Considered...'? What is their physical form? Are they written on paper or scratched onto cyber-space or recorded in some other format? Do they contain notes/thoughts on the film itself or on your day-to-day life or on existence in general or on all of these or none of them?

You write of how the film was interrupted 'half way through.' Did the footage of that first-shot half remain in the finished film, or did you begin again from zero when you resumed work?

There is so much pain in this story – and a terrible joy, too. I still feel confused in the presence of it all, and am hoping to find some way to... what? Not to comprehend, but to love it, I suppose. Your illness, the double loss of Samantha Berger, and, ultimately, the devastation of your daughter's death. These difficult things are all somehow part of your film – are the source of its innocent power for me – and I am certain that I will never understand them all. But, again, I hope that perhaps, better than understanding, I will be able to love them. Does that make any sense?

When you write, 'And I had also lost NINA of the Bambis,' I don't understand what you mean. Could you explain this to me, please?

I have not yet read 'The Risen,' but I would enjoy having the opportunity to do so.

You write: 'It has not been an easy journey' – which is clearly true. But I think it has probably been a necessary one, which somehow (in my mind, at least) makes it all alright. But maybe this is the Julian of Norwich in me: sharing her mantra in every breath: All shall be well and all shall be well and all manner of thing shall be well.

Just after I write these lines, I suddenly discover that T.S. Eliot arrived here long before me, in the fourth of his 'Four Quartets':

Whatever we inherit from the fortunate
We have taken from the defeated
What they had to leave us—a symbol:
A symbol perfected in death.
And all shall be well and
All manner of thing shall be well
By the purification of the motive
In the ground of our beseeching.

...as usual, I don't understand what he means. But I love it, all the same.

I send blessings on your head of white, and every hair thereof.

Peace,
j

correspondence considered...
Thursday, April 8, 2010 10:27 PM
From: "john sorensen"
To: "Peter Whitehead"

p,

i met with paul in washington square this afternoon and we discussed a possibility: that the proposed article on 'terrorism considered' that paul has asked me to write might take the form it is already taking: that of the e-mail correspondence you and i have been sharing (and, i hope, will continue to share) concerning the film, the book and a thousand other things.

he liked the idea, and i believe he's already mentioned it to you. to my mind, this approach is much more likely to result in something beautiful and worthwhile than any notes i would come up with on my own.

as well, i like the thought of the article beginning to be composed with the composers unaware of its composition.

what thinkest thou?

peace,
j

Re: correspondence considered...
Friday, April 9, 2010 5:20 PM
From: "Peter Whitehead"
To: "john sorensen"

dear John

Wonderful idea. I just hope that I don't now become SELF-conscious and edit much more than hitherto.

I would at some point need to see what I wrote to you about Samantha and Robin – before it was used. I am sure I will say ok. I am close enough to death myself not to care about repercussions.

I have sent an email I wrote to Samantha Berger to Paul. Please ask him for it – 3 pages I wrote after I was struck down with the Reiter's Syndrome – and a month before she killed herself.

As to your previous email's question – I said I had "lost" Nina... I am prepared to talk about this later. Not now. Remind me later.

peter w x

ps. I don't like the word 'correspondence'... too posh... I'd prefer something more odd – like web dialogue... but much better than that. And more succinct.

Duo-loguing
Friday, April 9, 2010 8:03 PM
From: "john sorensen"
To: "Peter Whitehead"

Dear Peter,

Yes, a big danger with this idea is that the dialogue/duologue will become a too self-aware performance-piece – a preening in the virtual mirror – and lose its innocence and truth in the process. But perhaps there is a way in which we may be aware of our awareness and avoid the trap. I don't know.

In any case, I feel that it's best if we consider our on-going exchange as only a rough draft of something that is still taking shape: that we should write freely and even wildly, then put all the transcripts together and examine them with the willingness to remove or synopsize or add material as needed to help the final draft tell the truth ('Art is a lie that tells the truth' as Picasso may or may not have said). For now, may we simply continue to share thoughts about the film and the novel and whatever else occurs, and see what comes?

I accept your rejection of the term 'correspondence' – but, at the same time, I see my side of our conversation as being a series of 'heart responses' to your film and book (so, in a way, I am literally 'coeur-responding' to your work). But I'm happy to explore other terms. I don't know much e-terminology, and I worry about coining an expression that is too cute (I think of things like 'a dia-blog,' then shiver a bit).

A final note for now: in considering the e-duologue possibility, I recall the moment in 'The Catcher in the Rye' when Holden writes, 'What really knocks me out is a book that, when you're all done reading it, you wish the author who wrote it was a terrific friend of yours and you could call him up on the phone whenever you felt like it.'

In a way, this is the experience I had in watching 'Terrorism...' – a film that 'knocked me out' so that I wanted to put the Holden Principle into action: 'calling up' the author (on the internet) and sharing thoughts as with a friend. It's a beautiful experience, and one that I think many readers might enjoy in sympathy.

Peace,
John

my first trip

Sunday, April 11, 2010 11:22 AM
From: "john sorensen"
To: "Peter Whitehead"

Dear Peter,

I've just completed my first trip through the novel of 'Terrorism Considered...' and I'm feeling a bit stunned by the frank display of nakedness and confusion that I found there.

The final experience in the wilderness (at the book's end) is a disturbingly accurate account of what I'm going through in my own mind after having spent much of the past week living inside this difficult story... which is and is not the story of the film that shares its name.

Before reading the book, the film of 'Terrorism' felt to me like a self-contained, complete entity. Perhaps it still is. But now I can't think of the film and the book as wholly separate things. These two hugely disparate expressions of your core-theme begin to feel like unusual, necessary companions: they are, for me, Siamese twins (sharing so many qualities, connected at the title, yet still primarily distinct from one another). And now, on this sunny but chilly Sunday morning in Greenwich Village, it seems to me as if each of them has married a different bride, and they are now needing a bed (in my head) that will hold all four of them together.

I am curious and eager to return to the film, taking with me the many intertwined thoughts and impressions that I've collected from the book. I wonder what that next trip will be like?

By the way, in the midst of my week with your book, a friend gave me a scratchy old copy of Nico's l.p., 'Desertshore,' and I read the final pages of 'Terrorism...' while she sang 'The Falconer' (do you know that track?). It was an unintended, mysterious and haunting complement to the experience.

Thank you for allowing me to share this walk into your northern woods.

John

Re: my first trip
Sunday, April 11, 2010 5:45 PM
From: "Peter Whitehead"
To: "john sorensen"

Dear John

'What rough drafts now slouch towards an inner... Bethlehem... Byzantium... Mongolia...'? Yes we will continue to share our lapses from the prison house of reason [eg... The Prison whore-house of Reason?] and see what emerges in the violet light... So to speak.

But I should have warned you. Alas I did not.

Herewith the first truth that has not been revealed. There are three novels which I CALL MY nohzone trilogy – WHICH ARE PUBLISHED ON THE INTERNET. At www.nohzone.com. Ter etc... Natures Child and Girl on the Train. They are, for me, merely three parts of ONE novel – as are the 3 parts of the film, three parts of one film. Separate but not separate. Stand alone but essential to the others.

There is a 4th novel – And Death Shall Have No Domain Name 2 which is a novel a reader imagines he might have read while/if reading the 3 novels simultaneously. That is it is vertical – not horizontal!

So the novel you read does end in confusion if you assume it is the end... of "the story"... it is only one third the way through. End of Chapter One! You have two more to go!!

Ter etc becomes ever more clear as you read the next two novels – when all is revealed at the very end. I think the next two novels are much better – less baroque in style (slightly!) – more linear.

Here is the problem. My film started as a film I would make of the second novel – only. "Nature's child." In it Maria and Yoko commit the eco-assassination... in Cumbria – I started the film with my wife-of-the time Yelizaveta (liza) as Maria... she is still in it, as Marilyn, of course... but we needed a Japanese girl as Yoko. We couldn't find one.

I went to Vienna with my films at the Viennale – and met Samantha. A Peruvian journalist writing for a magazine called "GODARD" there... and writing a thesis on revolutionary cinema. Who looks totally Japanese. And i fell in love with her... her beauty, her mind, her political passions.

I was also Possessed by Vienna... at night... the trams. (Like those in Liverpool where I was born! – and Skolimowski's BARRIER) BUT BUT It was ALPHAVILLE – the perfect setting for a film. Natures Child was to be shot in Cumbria where the novel takes place. The Land of the Lake Poets.

And suddenly I saw the film as a kind of post-modern take on Alphaville... MS a kind of Eddie Constantine??

Alas... this would mean taking Liza to Vienna. Difficult. She was studying Tango and Psychology at Birkbeck College. I wanted Vienna and Samantha. I had already started filming with Liza in the UK – the scenes in the finished film which were shot for Nature's Child, not the finished film!

I sold my house to pay for the film – and went back to Vienna to film with Samantha and see what evolved. Most of the scenes with Samantha were shot in this period before Christmas 2009...

I decided that the plot would now be that MARIA – her accomplice – had disappeared. So Lenoir would not be seen? Yoko was searching for her. Her quest as much as Michael's. Maria would be virtual... never realised.

Then I met NINA while filming a "Who Killed Bambi" concert. The PERFECT Maria Lenoir! Kill off a girl in a script and then she appears!

Another dilemma! I had to abandon the film as a version of the second novel – use more of the first novel or just let the film evolve, which is what happened... and yet promise I would use Liza somehow, later, when I had shot with Sam in Vienna.

Nina was perfect in many ways... but didn't like to act. Couldn't act. Samantha couldn't act and hated acting even more. A travesty of authentic truth seeking. Liza was taking acting lessons in London and appearing in several plays. I wrote a short play for her to perform – "Klaus Kinski was my father". Too shocking to be seen they all said!!

Sam found me a flat which I rented for a year – and she moved into the second bedroom. And we launched into the film – Sam and Nina violently jealous of each other. BUT – Neither of them could "carry the message" of the film – neither could articulate words. Even though Nina had seen every Godard film six times! And had been in Freudian psycho-analysis at the Freud museum for ten years!

Yeah... I decided by now – new plot problem and life problem – I was in love with NINA. She would have to be given the privilege role in the film – too – and I'd try to balance the two girls' roles. Nina and I were very close... and suddenly...

KAPUT. I was dying in agony, crawling around the floor of my flat in my own vomit... The disease that had crippled me in 1968 was back. With a vengeance. Reiters Syndrome. Discovered by a Viennese doctor in Auschwitz!!!!

Samantha watched in dismay – helpless – and started to crack up. I was an ugly sight. Nina came with food and tried to help as best she could – equally distraught. I knew I had to get back to the UK. They both ended up taking me to the airport. Nina part way to the town terminal – in a car with Sam, picking me up from my flat – unable to stand – and then Sam came with me on the airport train. At the terminal saying goodbye to Nina – 'forever' – as far as I was concerned and she was concerned I broke down and wept and she did the same and we held each other weeping... for ages... just standing locked in each others arms. My whispering into her hair that I loved her... With Sam watching. (A scene from a movie?)

On the train Samantha didn't stop talking... "I had no idea you loved Nina so much!" I was too ill to deny it... She said she now knew what the Vision of Tiresias was... the Violet Hour... (we'd read Eliot and Rilke together...) everything, every fragment of perception and feeling so intense and ecstatic it could not be avoided – or borne. Face to face, not through a glass darkly... Voir pour voir et pas pour regarder... Never have I seen a girl so lit up... so ecstatic... as she took me to the airport – where we had a coffee before saying goodbye.

I said I would be back soon, and we would complete the film. It did not seem convincing – for either of us.

I never saw her again. I was told she had had a breakdown and gone back to Peru. The truth was kept from me... by Nina, when I met her, when I returned six months later... having only just survived. I did some filming with NINA. She said she would be Maria. She went to Patagonia... came back. And never answered my calls... Everyone said she had gone silent and disappeared. She did that from time to time. I found Sophie again (after a year, after a brief contact)... and she saved the film... She became the "thread" I needed.

The scenes with Liza/Marilyn I had shot before Vienna – and the interrogation-monologues – but when I was editing I was amazed how good and relevant they were – to a very different film by now.

SO – now we come to The Third NOVEL... "The Girl on the Train." It is a quite close plagiarism of Kawabata's novel – SNOW COUNTRY... where the focus in my novel, is on a girl called Yoko in his novel who is seen briefly, and then disappears...

MS goes there for a Centenary conference for Kawabata's death... he meets two girls... Miyako and Yoko... and the three of them enact a scene... which becomes a kind of sexual NOH play together... and... maybe it is not K who is dead and whose death is being celebrated? But is it MS who is dead? – this whole novel is the dream at his moment of death? Set in the northern mountains of Japan? The Rains of Cumbria become the blizzards of Japan?

Each of the three novels is one step closer to his actual death. The first novel was originally called "Operation Nohzone" – the one you read. Later it became... TER etc...

When I had nearly died in the malicious hands of Vienna and its fascinating women... I decided to call the film Ter etc... and the novel too. I published the novel as it was – on the Internet – in case the film was a success. The title is better for the film than the novel I suspect.

.......***** (an almost) PS.

Yes I know the Nico song. I have a first edition of the LP. 'Coeur-reponding?' Good one! I see my Baroque style is catching? Just make sure my madness does not become infectious!

best
peter

phenomenalisimo
Sunday, April 11, 2010 7:49 PM
From: "john sorensen"
To: "Paul Cronin"

paul,

i've just received a rather phenomenalistic (is that a word? if it wasn't before, it is now) letter from peter, telling/sketching out the bizarre erotic-involvement-books-into-film-into-films-into-book background tale of 'terrorism...'

curiouser and curiouser.

i have no idea where all of this is leading, but it has already evolved into a strange and unique document – a kind of 'portal (into the mind) of the artist as an old man,' if i can twist joyce a bit.

peace,
j

whelmings
Sunday, April 11, 2010 8:27 PM
From: "john sorensen"
To: "Peter Whitehead"

p,

your latest letter has thoroughly whelmed [transitive verb: 'to turn (as a dish or vessel) upside down'] me.

thank you for sharing this intense map to hidden things – with its sketch of the tangled path of life-into-books-into-films-into-film-into-life-into-film-into-book, etc. that 'terrorism...' has traveled.

i'm in the midst of some new work on the sudan film just now, and it may take me a while to assess and respond to your notes, but i hope to do these things soon. in the meantime, i'd like to return to an earlier question: have you spent any time with martin buber's 'i and thou'? does his work interest you at all?

other things: one of my oldest and closest friends is lee underwood, the lead guitarist who worked with tim buckley on the original version of 'song to the siren,' and on most of buckley's early music. that song has been an important one in my life, and i feel happily haunted to come across it time and again in 'book one' of the trilogy.

thank you for this thing, too.

whelm on,
j

Re: whelmings
Sunday, April 11, 2010 9:12 PM
From: "Peter Whitehead"
To: "john sorensen"

j.

Take your time. It just flowed out.

No, Buber never crossed my path – except in a book by David Holbrook on Sylvia Plath and another he wrote on Dylan Thomas. He was a Buber man... but I never got caught.

Yes... I cannot listen to Song of the Sirens without weeping – especially now. If I do decide to kill myself (as I once did, walking into the sea) – that song will be with me. I also thought the version done by "This Mortal Coil" was excellent. So many sad tales... his death and his son's death.

Maria Lenoir I saw as some kind of Siren... swimming in the oceanic seductive waves of the webnets, the virtual images on screens... (but Maria was the name of my Ghost in my flat when I lived in London) – I will elaborate on that in some distant moment... not in the mean mean-while...

From now on I respond to YOU asking me questions about the film – or novel. Otherwise you will drown in all my Oceanic nightmares... that way we may keep it focused. You ask – I Coeur-respond. But don't forget I have two broken hearts to contend with. My real one... crhnic (oops – chronic I meant, maybe cthonic was trying to creep in)... heart failure. And that broken heart, from which there is no bipass... the death of my daughter Robin.

p.

know

Sunday, April 11, 2010 9:33 PM
From: "john sorensen"
To: "Peter Whitehead"

Dear Peter,

Please know that I never forget – and that, sometimes, the only things that I can remember are – those two broken hearts. More or less, this is why I write.

Peace,
j

through a draft, roughly
Tuesday, April 13, 2010 9:03 PM
From: "john sorensen"
To: "Peter Whitehead"

Dear Peter,

I'm thankful that you didn't warn me in advance about the interconnectedness of the three (or four?) novels and the film – I had a beautiful experience wandering into the maze unaware. Some trips are best taken without guide or map.

You write of the multiple elements of 'Terrorism...' (the books and film) as being 'Separate but not separate. Stand alone but essential to the others.' And I wonder: do you feel that it's important for the audience of the film to read the trilogy of novels? Or, the other way 'round, for the readers of the books to see the film? If these elements are 'essential' to one another, then they must be taken together, mustn't they? (The ceiling of Giotto's Scrovegni chapel in Padova is beautiful all by itself, but it wouldn't be up there to see without the walls to hold it in place.)

Also: is the '4th novel' a thing of words and plot and character – or is it entirely a concept in the mind of the author and/or reader? And how would I be aware of this 4th novel except through the rumor of it that you shared in your recent letter? If you hadn't told me directly of the 4th novel, would I ever know that it exists (does it exist)? I wonder, too, about related mysteries such as the short ('too shocking to be seen') play 'Klaus Kinski was my father,' which you wrote for Liza. Is there anything in that text which connects to the multi-plex 'Terrorism...' or is it a detour that leads elsewhere/nowhere?

You write, 'So the novel you read does end in confusion if you assume it is the end... of "the story"... it is only one third the way through. End of Chapter One! You have two more to go!!'

I accept that I have 'two more to go,' but, at the same time, I would like to clarify that my comment about 'the frank display of nakedness and confusion' that I felt in the book wasn't referring to the end scene of Novel One. I found the ending of that volume to be quite simple, clear and satisfying. In other words, I found this scene to be a lucid outward expression of the inner confusion being experienced by the character in it. It was the character's confusion that felt to me like a useful analogy for another mixed-up-ness that I was feeling: a more general sense of confusion that, for me, permeates the entire book. It isn't a confusion created by a lack of information or by authorial clumsiness, but one that seems necessary to the subject of the novel... which, for me, is not the plot, but the author. Does that make any sense?

When I live in your films and books, I feel something like an 'abundance of confusions' that is somehow central to my very positive (if not always comfortable) experience of them.

In my on-going times with the various entities that may or may not be 'Terrorism Considered...' there are several key elements that touch me deeply. I'm not certain precisely what they are, because I experience them (for the most part) viscerally and emotionally, not intellectually. But I know they are there. I feel them. When I ask myself to free-associate a response to the 'Terrorism' set, the terms that come to me are:

beauty, confusion, fear, confession, plea, pleasure, bewilderment... and woman, woman, woman.

Is there a political element in the set, as well? It may be that there is, but that I'm color-blind to it. Of course, I recognize the plot elements that have political connotations, but – for me – the 'Terrorism...' books/film are the work of a creator who is not a political artist, but one who is... what? Perhaps a 'political emotionalist' (I think of the way you describe your response to Samantha's 'political passions' when first meeting her). This connnectedness of politics to passion/emotion (with passion/emotion as the dominant element) is the feeling that always seems primary to me in encountering this work.

On the website for the upcoming Viennale screening of 'Terrorism...' there is a message from you, saying that, in this film: '...I want to investigate the CIA's influence on English culture, which is based on misinformation. This new film is influenced by Thomas De Quincey's novels, "Confessions of an Opium Eater" and "Murder Considered as a Fine Art," and I would say that it is about fear and control, or better still, about the fear that the state spreads in order to control. After having destroyed the Third World now we are also destroying this planet. Gaia is now, rightly so, revolting.'

I accept all of that as having something to do with the film I watched, but, for me, these are elements that are the pretexts rather than the texts of the work.

Do you see 'Terrorism...' as a primarily political film?

Well, these are some of my thoughts for now. I'll only add to them a final question for a distant moment: What do you mean when you write 'Maria was the name of my Ghost in my flat when I lived in London'? I'm happy to wait to learn.

Peace,
j

Samantha
Wednesday, April 14, 2010 8:34 PM
From: "Paul Cronin"
To: "sorensen"

note PLW attached to 3 page letter from Samantha:

'After which she killed herself.'

Joy

Thursday, April 15, 2010 10:00 AM
From: "john sorensen"
To: "Peter Whitehead"

Dear Peter,

Last night, Paul shared with me – as you suggested he might – the letter that you wrote to Samantha shortly before her suicide.

This morning, I am filled with thoughts of your many great losses and pains, and I am remembering something that I once read about Bach. I don't insist on the specifics, which I may have confused over the years, but I believe the principle is true.

I saw once an entry that Bach made in his journal at the time of the death of his first wife. He wrote: 'Lord, please let me not lose my Joy.'

When I think of this, I remember, too, a line in a book by some spiritual writer or another, who said that the only two real sins in life are sloth and despair.

I don't think that Bach was being insensitive or selfish or even wanting to simply avoid the pain of grieving. I believe that he had the wisdom to know that he could not fulfill his purpose in life if he lost his Joy in life. That he could not fully honor the dead (or, in his belief, worship God) if he became disconnected from the experience of Joy that is at the core of his – and I believe all – true being: in sufferings as much as (or more than) in pleasures. In any case, that's how it seems to me.

Blessings,
John

Re: Joy
Thursday, April 15, 2010 11:30 AM
From: "Peter Whitehead"
To: "john sorensen"

Dear John

Your Ode to Joy... Beethoven's Ode (Schiller) came at the climax of his 9th SYMPHONY. Not, in fact, of a Requiem. I have spent my entire life listening to Requiems. What was I looking for? The organ in Ashville which I played every day for hours... for four years or more? There is joy in Verdi's operatic Requiem – but it is more a celebration of joy in music. Not life or death. And Mozart's finished and not finished. Only his life finished. Part 3 of my film is a Requiem – for Gaia – but for Samantha. Who, for me, embodied the spirit and hope and despair of Gaia at the present time. Maria the virgin? No, Gaia the Goddess... Isis... Venus... but destroyed now by MAN.

In Bach's time, you lost half your children – or more. Wives came and went. You lived close to real tangible death. And so you were prepared for it, always expected it – and learned to live with joy between these acts of God's cruel Will. Your emotions, your nervous structures... were accustomed to such losses. This is no longer the case. Nowadays we live in denial of death – in western culture it is taboo. Especially in England it seems to me. Less so in Catholic countries where there is more closeness to death...

Death has become taboo for us. Virtual... we have the Media saturated with it. As if it has taken it out of us and freed us... the Media cultivates heroes of death... always has done. Now it is Pete Doherty... not Hamlet... not Lear... not Oedipus... (they are banished to the unconscious – the underworld – Greek tragedy was death through and through and was clearly an entertainment... catharsis. Pain mostly, no joy...)

I am a Baudrillard man – a Derrida man. I see the modern Mass Media as greedily and corruptly hijacking "death" and making it palatable, saleable – a commodity that people can buy... consumable. McLuhan's vision also...

We are not expected to assume at any moment – however many risks are being taken – that your 27 year old daughter – strong motivated street-wise. So full of life and ambition to celebrate it – Adored by everyone. Will suddenly be erased as if by the flick of a switch. As in THE Fall... the camera pans away from 'him' in the flesh – to his face on the little Media screen – facebrain mind of dots – blue screen of death... until the tape runs out – click – and he is erased. Suddenly Robin (at my side so often while I was editing my film) – is suddenly erased. And with it – indelibly erased – is a whole complex web of embodied patterns of instantaneous reflex reactions – emotion and psychological – that are there as part of my Self "structure". Robin's death has wiped out a huge colossal amount of my self-protective involutes (de Quincey) – I am raw, naked. Every leaf that buds and flowers, every bird that comes to my garden for food... robins planning to nest... the sun on a bright day... all such previous triggers for joy! Are now the worst triggers for pain anguish – even terror. You know you can't cope. You must stand back... find a way to turn a blind eye... see through the glass darkly and not face to face – because that power can kill you. As Tiresias in The Waste Land knew too well... Your emotional immune system has been shredded.

There can be no joy. Now. At all. For me. I do not seek it. The first glimpse of something that expects or demands joy – is obliterated. It could induce an angina attack which could kill me, in minutes. I have been close... it is joy and life and pleasure that now stalk me... when time like a running grave is tracking me down... As I put out any normal innocent curious psychic pseudopodia – whatever it touches – good news or bad – is too intense. A flash of intense 'heat'... Instant withdrawal... withdrawal/ A dangerous word surely... yes... I was addicted to life. I am now inadvertently addicted to pain. I have tried to escape it. I cannot. Robin is not here to share my joy... for me to feel joy would be betrayal. Of Her. Of us. Our project. Together. Betrayal of love... As was the death of Samantha...

And I do NOT believe in God. Or religion let's say. No easy escape there in fanciful rituals and Fellini-designed costumes... I sense there are gods... like that brown God of rivers that Eliot acknowledged in a lapse, a pagan moment... The gods... they are the deep hidden river gods in the blood – to paraphrase Rilke. Pagan gods are dark gods. Face to face no dark mirrors... They reveal only unpalatable truth... life is dark. At times there is a patina, a veneer of joy... a fragile persona... but for someone like me... (more in my next email in answer to your last one) – BETRAYAL is the ONE TOTAL issue – always – of my work and life. Fear of it... joy always threatened me more than anything... but joy with nature can be never a betrayal. The role of betrayers... remains with people...

Betrayal by God... by my father's death... who turns out NOT to have been my real father... my real father who is unknown to me and can never be traced... That scene in Brighton Rock... she is in the telephone booth. Which I saw as an early teenager. It went very very deep... the cracked bent gramophone record... the bifurcated words... "I love you I love you I love... dot dot dot... Nora and... dot dot dot... click click click..." Graham Greene has often touched my nerves too harshly... GENET... Saint Genet... the man who dared to say it all... in brutal pagan poetry...

More later
peter w.

Re: Joy

Friday, April 16, 2010 2:32 PM
From: "john sorensen"
To: "Peter Whitehead"

Dear Peter,

I am trying to understand your letter on death, joy and betrayal. I have experienced much death and human destruction in my life, some of it very recently. But I have no sense that the loved persons who died have been 'erased.' Not from life in general and not from my own life.

In the life of nature, of Gaia, these persons have been transformed, not erased. In the natural world, nothing ever disappears. Everything simply changes.

And, in my own mind and spirit and actions, I feel that these dear ones continue to live in each choice I make and in the consequences of those choices.

I would not and could not have responded to 'Terrorism...' as I did without those death-touched lives functioning so vitally and actively within my own life. I respond to you and your work because of those others. With them.

I definitely know the feelings of being 'raw, naked' that follow, like after-shocks, the earthquake of death in our lives. But I do not know the experience of having the beauties of life (the nesting birds, the shining sun) being seen as triggers for pain or terror. For me – at least so far – this has not occurred.

It is difficult for me to comprehend what you are describing. You write: 'There can be no joy. Now. At all. For me. I do not seek it... it is joy and life and pleasure that now stalk me... BETRAYAL is the ONE TOTAL issue – always – of my work and life. Fear of it... joy always threatened me more than anything... but joy with nature can be never a betrayal. The role of betrayers... remains with people...'

And there is so much that I don't understand.

Are people not part of nature?

Peace,
j

Re: Joy
Friday, April 16, 2010 5:36 PM
From: "Peter Whitehead"
To: "john sorensen"

Dear John

Had I been speaking to you about Samantha's death – before that of Robin, I think I would have answered everything very differently. And don't forget I made the whole of the Terrorism Film without knowing of Samantha's death. And it began as Nature's Child... Maria was Nature's Child... (Isn't there also a song of that title by Nico or someone similar? Nick Drake?)

It is Robin's death that has erased something in ME. Something I could not have foreseen, and even now – its ruthless unforgiving intensity – I feel it as a kind of terror. Is not Terror always to do with a fear of death? And as in the present zeitgeist politically – created and exploited at times by the "powers that be". Wanting the people to be afraid... as Baudrillard said – of losing touch with reality. Once you have lost touch with the sacred all you have is reality. Fear of losing that as well? Terror...

I am talking passwords now. Access. Access codes. What I was trying to talk about – before, to you – and will try to talk about now – is access to the "spirit"... both within us and without. I talked a lot to Samantha (who was a Marxist) about poetry – eg mostly Eliot's The Waste Land. and Rilke. This might shock you?? A year ago I started a new novel, a dialogue between a father and a favourite daughter. He was aware he was dying and had gone off to the HEBRIDES TO WRITE A NOVEL – AN UP-

TODATE new novel to be entitled 2012. Obviously his starting point was 1984 – he was alone on an island in a cottage. With only the birds to talk to. The sea and mountains. Writing a difficult impossible novel... The daughter is in the city – she is young... early 20s... making a film. She is a student. She wants to make an up-to-date film about The Waste Land – as it is now. The two are therefore – a new 1984, a new The Waste Land. The entire novel consists ONLY!!!!!! of their emails to each other!!! Exploring which one of them might be in touch with the "spiritual" let's call it.

The daughter – Nora... is doing a Masters on Eliot... hence her desire to see the poem as a film. Images... film. HE... will only use words. The novel starts with her asking HIM questions – what is his take on the Eliot poem. This phrase... that line... He answers trying not to be despairing and cynical. But she notices that his answer – in the google mail emails – have all got the google proposed links... suggesting meaning and interpretations of her texts – in the mind of Google – at the right hand side of every one of their emails. GOOGLE's answers to her questions! (To the first question – hey dad what does this or that really mean?)... Google has an answer too. There was even a reference in my first two emails – believe it or not – to a website LINK about Djuna Barnes...

To cut a long story short... Eliot's The Waste Land – some say – would be meaningless without his added NOTES at the end. (Some say he added them to create more confusion!) In the NOTES he says the entire poem is meaningful only by seeing that it "is the world seen through the eyes of Tiresias"... he who as the androgynous Shaman sees that world of the violet hour...

The conceit of the novel is that their emails are hijacked by Google. She goes off following the Google links... asking less and less of her father... alone in his solitude. His isolation. As in Alphaville the Computer is the force that is moulding HER mind, her thesis, her work, her Being. More and more they are separated by the Google Notes – and her temptation to follow them up – they end up less and less discussing her difficulty in deciding what the poem really is about. She sees her task to write a Google Waste Land... Eliot's theory about Tiresias? Her father (wise old man)'s comments to his beloved daughter, are painful as he tries to comfort her, that she must live now and have to grow up in dumbed down "The Wasted Land". The waters of nourishment have dried up.

So what is The Waste Land in my film and present life context? For me – speaking now about access codes – it is the land (from ritual to romance qv) in which the sacred is NO LONGER ACCESSIBLE. I would agree that if there is anything "spiritual" – it must still be there (even if we go away it will still be there) and be part of all nature and be accessible to those who have the codes... birds worms plants bacteria... etc... as Eliot believed he had the codes... taking communion every morning of his life... but was more and more fearful they might elude him... sad about the mad wife... dying so young in her asylum... rich family?

The poem The Waste Land is about the death of "Gaia"... in the Lovelock self as well as the Greek myth about her being and life. The nourishing loving forces that have created life here; our lives and that of every living creature on the earth. DEATH within

US... because we have destroyed the codes. The natural codes of access. The "violet vision"... We may still be alive – but without access to the spiritual. Our modern world culture has erased those access codes. The spirit is indeed in those birds in my garden... I spent over twenty years in the desert "being a bird"... Horus, son of ISIS/GAIA... trying to breed falcons that were either poisoned in their nests and food, or hunted by greedy humans.

That novel – my ELIOT novel – I discussed a lot with Robin. It was based on Robin and I... Much more recently than with Samantha long ago. There are quite a few references in my film to TIRESIAS though... as I was editing it – not suspecting Samantha was already dead and Robin would die one month after she came to the Opening in Paris with me – December 12th. She dies on the 24th January. Mostly the references were mine in the film obviously – but also because Samantha was fascinated by "the Vision of Tiresias" (the title of one of my former unfinished works... a screenplay treatment... also called The Hooded Falcon... he is of course blind, no sight, only insight... a novelist and poet, not a film-maker??) – That vision Sam felt as ecstasy... ek stasis – and a threat. Clearly it was. It sucked her out of being human, no longer restrained and in control – she tried to fly, to become a bird... an angel probably... only to die seconds later, unable to fly...

In the film "Nothing to do with me" – is there not a tale (true) about someone who throws him/herself off the Notre Dame Cathedral in Paris?? I think you should see that film – to see that I have been at the threshold of the Violent Vision for a long long time... why am I still here? It is so odd.

The vision of Tiresias... the adversary of Oedipus. Of Reason. For me the most important experience in my life was the "work" I did with a Shaman in Pakistan. For 18 months... he PROVED to me without a shadow of doubt that there are dimensions in which there is something we have given the name – the "spiritual" – but he even proved it to be tangible. I have the tangible proofs... That is another whole story... the subject of a 250 page book I am trying to complete – "Once Out of Nature..." qv Yeats Byzantium...

So. Before the death of Robin I would have said I COMPLETELY accept the existence of that other dimension... it is referred to a lot in my novels. Especially in The Risen – I call it The R Field. The Risen is about this very subject. The teachings of Kamal Sahib became totally true to me in my later life... as he proved them to have been in my previous life... one day I will tell you of them.

In my film – there is Samantha... such a premonition – or was I responsible? (Heart of Glass!)... Samantha talks of angels... implying talk of death. Hearing of her death just two weeks before my final actions in completing my film – the titles! – devastated me. The film was originally a Requiem for Fernando Pereira the eco-terrorist. So I changed it – for them both.

But her death did not erase my access codes... her death, on reflection, seemed so ordained, so inevitable... it really was to seek peace... shantih shantih shantih... after the terror of the ecstasies that she felt and lived every minute of every day. You would say of her... Samantha simply had to die! She saw, like Webster, death beneath the skin...

Robin? No-one you could meet was more – Given to Life... as Robin. There were depressions and lapses of course. But not for a second could you have foreseen or even imagined her dying. I have earlier emails from Samantha in which you see her flying close to the eye of the storm... the cyclone...

For Samantha, the world had become The Waste Land. For Robin... she was still living in hope... exploring the ecstatic visions of The Lake Poets... the Ancient Mariner... The Prelude... De Quincey... those for whom the natural world and every aspect of life was tangible and ecstatically beautiful (have you seen the film PANDAEMONIUM. We watched it together. A masterpiece.) Another masterpiece. We also watched Edvard MUNCH by Peter Watkins. She watched it twice alone afterwards. She did a lot of painting... photography... films... music... poetry...

I was that broken man alone in a cottage in a desolate Hebridean island... (Scotland was my first Hunting ground for falcons... I bought a cottage there once... high in the mountains... then Morocco...) My character in the novel is desperately trying not to be hurt, and to hurt, watching his daughter... as things fall apart... the centre unable to hold... (her mind being diluted by the trash links – The Notes – created by Google.)

With Robin's death – when she died something in me died too. You say there is no death in nature. All is transformation. TRANS – FORM – ation. FORMS change... Once she was a living body. Living in our weird holographic past-future time. Now she is dust. Her previous form has been erased... it no longer exists... that is undeniable. And what was in me – that belonged to her... that opened my eyes through her eyes... no longer exists.

As I said – Kamal Sahib's work with me taught me there WAS/IS a spiritual dimension and you COULD/CAN communicate with it. He taught me to do so – we did it together. I have PROOF of all this... notebooks that go back fifty years... his visions going back to Ancient Egypt. As the 'Ancients' knew and felt... I have been there – in that TIRESIAN state... often enough... and it is painful and terrifying when it gets out of hand.

So Eliot wrote his poem saying all this... ie ONCE we had access to the "gods"... and in 2000 years we have lost that access more and more... that wave-field is still there and we try new methods to reach it – as he suggested in The Four Quartets.

I still had the codes when I made the film... despite sensing I was close to death as I am indeed close to death... still hoping I could communicate some tangible perception of these "more than"... domains... I wanted to make a film in the spirit of Eliot... As HE had made The Waste Land I wanted to make my film... (too bad the audience might NOT be convinced by my Requiem for Film... Requiem for the eyes and vision of TIRESIAS.)

My fear all along (which is why I gave up film and went for 25 years into the desert with my falcons – those with the Horus Magical eyes – the Third Eye...), my FEAR and desperate certainty has always been that FILM/photography... that primitive instinct it stole – eats the soul... (Fear eats the soul

– Fassbinder)... My Film THE FALL... what is The Fall? rejection from Eden... from Paradise. Paradise is Tiresias.

I was aware while making my TER FILM that it might be a lie. That film CANNOT EVER be "spiritual" in that sense... by its very nature it corrupts and steals the spirit. Hence the zeitgeist of the present world... The Waste Land... Gaia mourning the murder of her daughters... the nymphs and goddesses... The Midsummer Nightmare...

I was fearful I was faking it and telling a lie... but I was trying! Trying to give some sense of wonder... never sure. So that is why the subject of the film is UNCERTAINTY DELUSION DISIN-FORMATION MISINFORMATION BETRAYAL... those referred to in my previous email and answers, I hope, to your questions... Clearly I touched you with my film, and I am touched that I did so. Time might reveal as to why you were touched. I fear I may only have tricked you.

That was Robin... puck... the trickster... Robin's death killed me too. I am living Yeats' "Death in life" – which quote I think he got from Blake. or Shelley or Keats? Nothing that would once have been a hypertext link to the spiritual... a yellow hammer male chasing off another male in my garden and the demure female watching watching the fight... none of the old links can "touch" me now... No! Rather they DO touch me – as I said – but in the opposite negative sense. They do not provoke joy. They each provoke instant pain – terror – yes, it provokes terror. My film title was only to become so painfully apt...

Because Robin is not here to SHARE... anything and everything... I can feel only pure pain... so harsh I fear it will switch off my heart.

The domains of the spiritual are indeed still there because nature itself and humans with all their faults still have access to it in various forms... weaker and weaker... inadvertently at times... but I have lost the codes. As in Alphaville! I feel like Darwin, so destroyed and forever... after the death of his beloved daughter... the daughter is dangerous. The anima. The Soul. The psycho-pomp who is the CODE by which access is gained to the Spiritual... How Oedipus becomes Tiresias... using the eyes of his daughter Antigone! I have lost my Antigone... I am now merely a tattered coat upon a stick... Crazy jane said it all... she'd met the Bishop in the lane... I have lost my crazy jane... I made a film called DADDY... because of Sylvia Plath's poem... her loss of her father. This time, as I never assumed it could ever be... it has become inverted.

I am alone on my island... waiting for the cliff to crumble...

peter

PS Don't forget to change your emails to me – from a new google account? – so you can see what Google makes of our references, texts, and notes.

(mo)Re: Joy

Saturday, April 17, 2010 1:50 PM
From: "john sorensen"
To: "Peter Whitehead"

Dear Peter,

Your letter has touched me more deeply than I have words to say. I know that I will not be able to properly write what is in my heart, but I send this message to you as some kind of symbol/indicator of what is going on within me.

I only know of two ways to communicate – two ways that, for me, are one way: to love and to pray. These are the only things that I know how to do, and so I do them as best as I am able. No matter what else I say or don't say to you, today or ever, I am offering this love and prayer for you always, because... does there have to be a because?

I have been reading the autobiography of St. Thérèse of Lisieux ('The Story of a Soul'), and your letter has made a connection for me with one short section in her book, near the end. She writes of something that she experienced not long before her death: a time when 'pitch-black darkness' swept over her soul, destroying all her peace and torturing her. She says, 'I wish I could express what I feel, but it is impossible. One must have travelled through the same sunless tunnel to understand how dark it is.' All through her life, she had sensed the existence of something joyful and perfect and right: 'a new world.' '...Then, quite suddenly, the mists which surrounded me sank into my soul and smothered it so that I could not even picture this lovely country... everything about it had vanished!'

I don't understand these devastations, but I recognize them. And when I read your letters, I have a longing to... what? I don't know. Do I sound like a fool if I say 'to help'? I don't mind sounding or being foolish – if only this truth may be useful.

I feel to respond to your letter in a haphazard way. We'll talk passwords... or passsentences or passparagraphs. I hope this is alright. A few things:

Do you know of John Lennon's unreleased song, 'Child of Nature'? I believe that it was written during the trip to India in '68.

There are so many important things in your letter. Things which help me to better understand what you've written in other letters – in the transparent words of your letters and books, and in the glowing images on your screens.

'It is Robin's death that has erased something in ME.'

This makes complete and terrible sense to me, and seems to be very connected to the idea that follows soon after: 'Once you have lost touch with the sacred all you have is reality.'

This is the message that, more than any other, draws me to your work and to you. (Who do I know? You or the work or one in the other or a reflection in the river?) At the heart of this whateveritis connection is a feeling I have of a person who has been bitten by the hounds of both heaven and hell. (A bite is a kind of touch, isn't it?)

'What I was trying to talk about – before, to you – and will try to talk about now – is access to the "spirit"... both within us and without.'

This is the subject that interests me most of all in the father who has 'only the birds to talk to. The sea and mountains.' And, most especially, through the exploration he shares with his daughter as to 'which one of them might be in touch with the "spiritual."'

I feel certain that, no matter what else has been 'erased,' this exploration of spiritual touches is still going on. Somehow or other. I don't insist. I don't have a right to insist. But it's what I feel.

I am remembering something: 'Devi (the Goddess who becomes incarnate as Parvati) says: "Ever since I killed myself, Shiva has thought of me constantly, unable to bear his separation from me. He wanders naked, and has become a yogi, abandoning his palace, wearing unconventional clothing. Miserable because of me, he has abandoned the highest pleasure that is born of desire. He is tortured by longing and can find no peace as he wanders everywhere, weeping and behaving like a lover in distress."'

I don't believe that Google exists. I accept that it 'appears to exist' and that, in my dream of it, I utilize it (and perhaps I am somehow utilized in the process) in various ways. But my intuition is that Google-Alpha-60 is an illusion (from the Latin, illusio, meaning 'the action of mocking'; from illudere, meaning 'to mock at'). In our Alphaville, maybe the machine is mocking us only as long as we believe in the illusion: until Natasha can say (and begin to mean) "Je vous aime."

What do you think of Cocteau's 'Orphée'?

You write, 'The waters of nourishment have dried up.' And I write, 'Until it rains again.' And, in my small experience, it always rains again. Even if it only comes when we are sleeping.

'*...So what is The Waste Land in my film and present life context? For me – speaking now about* *access codes – it is the land in which the sacred is NO LONGER ACCESSIBLE. I would agree that if there is anything "spiritual" – it must still be there (even if we go away it will still be there) and be part of all nature and be accessible to those who have the codes... birds worms plants bacteria... etc...'*

And, I feel, to us: though maybe mostly when we are sleeping. And perhaps especially when we are still a bacteria or plant or worm in the womb, and an unfledged bird at the breast.

'...*We may still be alive – but without access to the spiritual. Our modern world culture has erased those access codes.'*

And yet – for me (and I do insist on this, because I am experiencing it even as I write), your letters still contain those erased codes. How can this be? Am I delusional or is it possible that there may be some kind of code beyond the codes – something that is more than a 'code'... something which may be communicated with the instrument of communication being unaware? ('...if there is anything "spiritual" – it must still be there.')

Yes, there is a tale in 'Nothing to do with me' about the woman who throws herself off the Notre Dame Cathedral. When I remember it, I suddenly wonder if there is some connection between that story and the parable of 'The Appointment in Samara.'

You write of Samantha that 'her death did not erase my access codes...' but that 'With Robin's death – when she died something in me died too. You say there is no death in nature. All is transformation. TRANS – FORM – ation. FORMS change... Once she was a living body. Living in our weird holographic past-future time. Now she is dust.'

Do you feel that a person and the form they appear to take are the same thing? Was Robin only the form that she took in the time that you knew her? Was she a living body? Is she dust? These things don't make sense to me. What does make sense to me is when you add: '...Kamal Sahib's work taught me there WAS/IS a spiritual dimension and you COULD/CAN communicate with it... I have been there – in that TIRESIAN state... often enough... and it is painful and terrifying when it gets out of hand.'

There is the terror again.

You write, 'film CANNOT EVER be "spiritual"... by its very nature it corrupts and steals the spirit.'

Does film – or any material thing – have a nature beyond the functions we call it to serve? To put it in other terms: Is the bread or wine of communion spiritual before it has been blessed? Might it be possible to bless the film before shooting it or showing it? I don't know. I'm wondering.

You write 'I was fearful I was faking it and telling a lie... but I was trying! Trying to give some sense of wonder... never sure.'

I read these words and I feel that maybe I start to know you. Certainly I feel a greater admiration and love for you – a relation. Because trying is all I am able to do.

'...Clearly I touched you with my film, and I am touched that I did so. Time might reveal as to why you were touched. I fear I may have only tricked you.'

Love isn't a trick. Pleasure may be, but not love.

Also: I don't want to see 'what Google makes of our references, texts, and notes'! I like our letters just as they are: linkless and naïve (feminine of naïf, from Old French, 'inborn, natural').

Also-also: One last password from Lisieux's Thérèse:

'I know that without love all we do is worthless.'

Peace,
j

Re: (mo)Re: Joy
Sunday, April 18, 2010 5:55 PM
From: "Peter Whitehead"
To: "john sorensen"

Dear John

I think we have drifted too much into a discussion of my present emotional predicament. triggered by Robin's death. In the true sense, Robin was not involved in the making of the film – as to its form or content or purpose. She was my loyal technical assistant. It was only when I asked her to type out the narratives that she really looked closely at the film. Although she did see it at the Cinematheque showing on 12 December.

I would like to return more to talking about the Film – and the related novel – and perhaps the other two linked novels. The film really IS a "precis" let's say of three (4!) long novels. The film is a kind of plagiarism of them I think! I think you might be searching for (and I hope finding) some sources of my film – yes – but perhaps some explanations of its "mystery" and why the film should have touched you. There may indeed be clues in the three novels. There are for me of course – thousands – but for a viewer of the film – totally unnecessary.

You must and will reveal YOURSELF in revealing what you have seen and felt in watching the film. Being EXPOSED (sic) to it. Just as James Riley (as you have seen), being someone who thinks more like Paul, than you and I – we who see the invisible as much (if not more) than the merely visible? – as James Riley also reveals himself in the way he has written about the film. Much more linear/rational. I think his approach will be that of the majority who might ever see the film, if we get it to become an available DVD.

For me the film was a kind of 'poem'... to use words and images in it, the way certain poets use their words... to create an experience in the imagination. As I think I have said – it is hard if not impossible with FILM to achieve the NUMINOUS... impossible! By definition. It can do other things... Cocteau and Bunuel, Tarkovsky... yes there are others. The numinous...

So. Cocteau and Orphee. Yes indeed, yes indeed. By some very odd quirk – my very first film, while I was a new student at the Slade School of Art – having decided to make a film (or two) for the Christmas student party! I made a ten minute film, shot with a gang of motor bike boys and others, in Clacton on Sea!! – which was a mini pastiche of the Cocteau film. (I then later did the same with Last Year in Marienbad, shooting it in the Slade School AGORA of Greek Classical Monumental buildings! The two films were condensed into one – now called the Theft. A typical student film!! Awful...)

I saw Orphee when I was at school – engulfed in Tschaikovsky and the Methodist Hymn book and Verdi and Italian Opera (my versions of)... in my capacity as film organist – and in love with one of the matrons – 18 year-old Gypsy girl Norma Whiteley – whence my choice of name – NORA! My first great passion, love and betrayal – my first lived Greek tragedy! It was indeed the second film in my life that possessed my soul – and stayed with me forever. The first was "Sister Carrie" – based on the Dreiser novel – with Laurence Olivier and Jennifer Jones. (Does Nina not look like Jennifer Jones?)... As is described by Giandomenico CURI – whose purpose in his article – very very very important to me, as far as I am concerned! – his purpose is to take the films that I have claimed at differing times and in differing contexts – to have been my sources. Ending with Alphaville... Pierrot le Fou... etc He has shown that in EACH of these films there is a common denominator... they are relevant to me – to my story... (qv a text I sent to Paul called "A Tale of 3 Cities!" I think it was. Just a first take...)

As James Riley has found in all my written novels. This same "involute" as De Quincey calls it. I was never conscious of it – but now that you have asked about this Cocteau film, I can say that the TER film is very much suggestive of that trip down into the underworld in search of Eurydice... and the Voices heard from the "R Field" – as I called it in my novel The Risen – in the film are those emails sent to the girls by Maria Lenoir (my Eurydice). The influence is very tangential – more a "mood" that is there. That someone like yourself might feel. Detect. Resonate with. Certainly it is not in any sense part of the film's direct meanings... to an average audience. (If it ever receives such an audience?)

I do not and cannot expect you to read 'The Risen' – especially for this Framework project. It is a long novel. BUT one of the essential "conceits" of it is that two (re)searchers conduct experiments at the same instant in two differing places. A physicist in Cambridge working with a pyramid-shaped diamond crystal from ancient Egypt – and John Faulkner – a psycho-pharmacologist/hippie into chemical transformation of consciousness – each unaware that the other is there and is (in modern parlance) entangled with him... (Entanglement was not discovered when I wrote the novel)... After the joint but separate experiments, Matthew in his lab is mysteriously possessed... and has to follow his dreams now, rather than his reason... reason eludes him more and more as he follows his calling, the quest now made for him... but John totally disappears. (All this is the work of a Shaman, Amenhotep from the 18th Dynasty of AE!... who enters into the time and space of the two experiments with his inputs)... the novel is about how these two real (and a 3rd maybe virtual) consciousnesses come to fuse – were maybe always fused – perhaps they are all parts of the one person. Myself? The point is that Matthew starts receiving communications from John... even to the point of being drawn down to Cornwall where he gets involved with the two girls – who were John's lovers. One whom he meets by accident in the Fitzwilliam Museum in Cambridge.

He thus receives a long involuntary INITIATION – a kind of CROWLEY/MATHERS magical trance-formation by "messages" from John. They "come to him" from and across what I called 'The R Field'... some might now call it the 5th Dimension. Soon to be revealed in reality and fact by the discoveries in Holographic Time Space experiments... qv Maldecena. And Rodolfo Llinás working with Consciousness and the Brain.

John "transmits" to Matthew through/into Matthew's dreams... which he soon recognises are NOT his own. (THIS all comes from my work with Kamal Sahib). And through the contents of 13 encrypted computer discs (plus 1) that he finds in John's work room. They are all encoded. By listening to the dreams and interpreting them, he finds a way to unlock the codes and read the discs... which are the means by which Matthew is TRANCE – formed – and becomes initiated. But of course... he must die.

It is entirely based on, and is an interpretation of – the Legendary mythic story of the Isis Mysteries. Isis and Horus and Osiris. Not Orpheus and Eurydice... but of course they are linked. The stories/tales ARE precisely a description of Initiation into the Mysteries. As in the Eleusinian Mysteries. Demetra and Persephone...

That is my territory. SHAMANISM.

I bought a CD for her – I made Samantha listen to Cocteau's music/text etc for PERSEPHONE!!! with Stravinsky's music... he who did 'Oedipus Rex' of course. I also published the script of Pasolini's Oedipus Rex in my Lorrimer Screenplays series.

You say you 'use Love and Prayer.'

I have loved, oh yes I have loved – and been dismembered and uplifted by it. But I have never prayed. I see it as meaningless for me. BUT I use techniques of Shamanism... as did Kamal Sahib. Much closer to Meditation I suppose... just letting go. And my novel The Risen is the "inner story of the Falcon Horus" – in my life. I bred falcons in the Falcon centre. But I bred falcons in my soul also...

No – you cannot help in the sense that you can reach my pain – offer any kind of cures... no... that VOID so perfectly described by that wise Priestess... in your email. Those wonderful ecstatic doomed Christian Mystics... one of whom is celebrated in Rilke's Duino Elegies in the first elegy I think... Gaspara Stampa... her letters! His Elegies for the death of a young girl... Persephone... Samantha... Eurydice...

But you help me in the essential way – the very best and most directly nourishing way – by celebrating my film. My work. My sacrifices... because you know only too well, I sense, what goes into such work. Such Shamanistic texts and film... By seeing in it what is hidden... and thus showing that I am NOT alone! And not merely insane. Not entirely alone in my misery now... possessed by that void... that ennui that has stalked me always, in truth... since my father died probably, when I was eleven – as Freud said – the very worst thing that can happen to a male child... (Those ghosts that must stalk every shaman. It is the nature of shamanism to be torn to shreds. Into 13... and maybe 14 parts)... Exhausted!

best wishes and peace to you too.
peter.

PS. Google does exist. As did Alpha 60. And Godard's MIND... Google has just read this email, now that you have received it – as it read yours to me – and advised me on suitable links! eg "Visit the Orpheus Bar" in Lower Manhattan, The Bowery. Happy Hour Sundays 5pm to 5am!!"... or... "Buy the New Holographic T-Shirts from ORPHEUS RETAILERS INC – at 151 Broadway. The Abasement. Also Buy the Green Lasers with which to view them."

peter w.

Re: (mo)Re: Joy
Monday, April 19, 2010 10:17 AM
From: "john sorensen"
To: "Peter Whitehead"

Dear Peter,

A film, in and of itself, may not be able 'to achieve the numinous' – but isn't it possible for that film (like any other thing) to be a vehicle of the numen (Latin, 'nod,' 'divine will'; akin to Latin nutare 'to nod': 'a spiritual force or influence often identified with a natural object, phenomenon, or place')?

I once read a short reminiscence by a scientist who described the key 'numinous' moment in his life. He recalled being a child of 6 or 7 years of age, sitting in a math class, when the teacher explained the concept of 'zero.' He said that he couldn't sleep that night, haunted by the thought that this thing, this '0,' was a thing that was nothing – that a thing existed which, when added to another thing, had no effect on the other. Something like that. He said he felt that the teacher's zero was the trigger for a numinous moment that changed him profoundly, and led him onto his life-path of mathematics, physics, science... and more: that it helped him to begin to know who he was.

Can't a film do something similar? What happened within you when you first saw 'Sister Carrie' or the Warsaw Ghetto film? Weren't those numinous experiences?

I agree that 'Terrorism...' (the film) is, as you say, 'a kind of poem' – and, for me, a true poem is a thing that is a numen/nod of the greatest and most useful/meaningful kind.

I've asked Paul to show me the Italian 'PW' book, and I hope to see it soon.

Do you remember your first thoughts on 'Sister Carrie'? How old were you when you saw that film – and where were you? Did the novel have a strong impact on you as well, or only the film?

I haven't seen that film (or read the novel) in many years, but in my memories of it – and thinking of 'Terrorism...' (film), as well – I wonder if you see in Carrie/Jones (remembering Jennifer Jones' difficult relationship with Robert Walker, and the twisting crash/turns of his post-Jones life) some kind of natural-born eco-terrorist: a precursor of Maria Lenoir, aspiring to love, inspiring devotion... and destroying in the process. Does that sound absurd?

Thank you for sharing this much of 'The Risen' with me: '...Matthew in his lab is mysteriously possessed... and has to follow his dreams now, rather than his reason... reason eludes him more and more as he follows his calling, the quest now made for him... but John, totally disappears... the novel is about how these two real (and a 3rd maybe virtual) consciousnesses come to fuse – were maybe always fused – perhaps they are all parts of the one person. Myself?'

For this much alone, the novel is beautiful for me.

You say, 'I have never prayed. I see it as meaningless for me. BUT I use techniques of Shamanism... as did Kamal Sahib. Much closer to Meditation I suppose... just letting go.'

Could you explain for me the distinction in your mind between prayer and meditation? In one of the spiritual books that I read many years ago, the writer said something to the effect that he felt people in the West have a very wrongheaded idea of what prayer is. He said something like, 'We think that prayer is talking – is telling Someone or Something what we want, like making a grocery list and giving it to Santa Claus. But true prayer isn't a telling, it isn't even an asking – it is a listening.' I understood him to be saying that prayer is, as you say of meditation, a 'letting go.' An accepting of an invitation to a journey.

[Do you care for Baudelaire's 'L'invitation au voyage' – or for the musical setting of it by Henri Duparc?]

Viva Gaspara Stampa! – viva to dear Anaxilla and viva even to the thorn that made her bleed poetry and song; viva to, as you put it, all of 'what goes into such work.' Viva for seeing what is hidden, and viva to being 'NOT alone! And not merely insane. Not entirely alone in my misery now...'

I would like to read 'Nature's Child.' I spoke with Paul last night, and he said that he's happy to print out a copy for me. He asked that you send to him the files, so that he may print them as soon as possible. I'd like to read the novel before returning to watch 'Terrorism...' (film) again.

Yesterday I read Cocteau's script for 'Orpheus.' Following the screenplay, there was a note from Cocteau concerning the film. He concluded with:

'...time is a purely human notion and, in fact, does not exist at all.'

(Is Google more real than time?)

Peace for Peace,
j

Re: (mo)Re: Joy
Monday, April 19, 2010 9:43 PM
From: "Peter Whitehead"
To: "john sorensen"

Dear John

JS: A film, in and of itself alone, may not be able 'to achieve the numinous' – but isn't it possible for that film (like any other thing) to be a vehicle of the numen?

PW: I think only rarely – and maybe not. There is too much of the real (in a corrupted state) in a film/ed image – especially as it moves through time. It is never still...

Your other question illuminated my ideas a little.

The Carrie film – more later – The Warsaw Ghetto film – and Orphee (with a slight hesitation...) were indeed films that possessed me, as I use the word – and have stayed with me ever since. And may have influenced my ambivalent attitude to FILM. (very important you realise I did not like ANY of my films – except The Fall – but I think I achieved something totally different with the TER film – finally – by accident).

Those three films were NOT numinous. No! Not at all. Those films affected me in a very different sense – in the Jungian sense. In each of them I felt and partially recognised a PSYCHOLOGICAL and SOCIAL narrative and presence. They spoke to me because, archetypally – in the Jung sense – their archetypal structure resonated with my own – gave me the chance to come face to face with those inner structures – at that time in my life. I was simply NOT aware of them when I saw that film.

WE ARE FORMED ARCHETYPALLY at a very early age – as Freud proved time and time again. By the age of eleven I was hewn; like rock. Pierre. Never to be changed. As we all are. The only hope we have is of surrender to Individuation – Jung I much prefer – (to slough off the false self) – which is to BECOME conscious of our own particular UNCONSCIOUS.

Those films were entirely about the webs that entrap us – from within and without – as we struggle with fate – the structure that fate has imposed on us. eg Mother and Father, siblings... all this is social psychological... if we are crushed by these potentially 'terrible' forces that try to mould us like soft clay... we can only survive those hauntings by some process of (self) sacrifice... sacro facere... breakdown... psychoanalysis... initiation into one or another Mystery Play....... we must give up the ghosts that bind us, so we can give up the masks we have assumed to please them – in order to become finally free. Sometimes it amounts to murder. Or second best – self murder. God protect us from Family. qv Feud essays on Heimliche... the FAMILIARS...

Back to my 3 films above. In each there is a structure, as in a molecule, of competing negative and positive forces (eg Matthew John Cindy Georgina in the novel the Risen – the double pyramidal quaternio structure of a single person... they embody each of the archetypes... anima animus and so on.)

In Sister Carrie... Orphee... and oddly, the Warsaw Ghetto film... were differing fragments of a single plot. My plot. My myth. My destiny. Fight it and be crushed and die. Or get to KNOW IT! Become Conscious of your own Fractured Unconscious. Because it is always fractured. No-one is whole. We are born with the desire to be whole, with the instinct for it... but the story we inherit... me in the slums of Liverpool and an absent father who came back and promptly died... being stripped of all previous "structures"... uprooted and plunged... with wide open scared seeking eyes... into the Ghetto of a Public School created for Methodist Ministers Sons... 470 boys paid for by parents and me – by Clement Atlee. I was not finding it easy...

There is perception of deep deep meaning – and meaningful discourse with the experiences enacted – in this case of films... but for me it is nothing to do with the numinous. It is seeing yourself... as a social thinking person needing to know yourself... forever searching... le pelerinage... and such dramas (derived from which Greek word?) are mirrors offering therapy. (Narcissistic?)

"Le narcisse est le plus jole fleur du monde
Et celui qui pench sur son odeur
Vois le monde inconnu des enfers..."

Cocteau... in Stravinsky's Persephone...

This being possessed by a narrative film like Carrie... is not numinosity – for me. It does not demand that I pray... That's why I was so impressed by that Italian chapter that you will see, I hope. The writer had asked – 'Is there something similar in all these apparently differing films that PW says "possessed" him. If so... Why?' The answer was yes – he said – he saw each one as the essentially the same on that archetypal structural level.

All my novels deal with the same deep conflict that has made me. The father and the daughter... The Master and Marguerita!

I went to the desert and lived with Falcons. For 25 years. That too was an expression of my trying to deal with my MYTH...

Which obviously is 'Oedipus'. Orphee and Horus relate to the same pattern – or involute – of problems... the absent father. No-one has such an absent father problem as Jesus Christ! Never able to escape from the devouring powers of the Virgin Mother!? Hopkins' poem The Windhover – equates Horus and Christ. As he longs to be torn to shreds by Christ! Gash vermillion...

BUT BUT BUT... I do believe in the numinous. There are no words to express it, so why should I try? let me just say that I think the Surrealists were seeking this kind of heightened way of Seeing... especially Ernst... collage/montage... strategies to deconstruct linear rationality – and in the gaps left... the syncopes... you receive, directly, something that is beyond above outside of words or perception... intimations of immortality. There are huge gaps in the structures that comprise our Four Dimensional Space time continuum. (Which we perceive so well through and by Reason... Hence the certainty that so many researchers in so many fields (wave fields) have of the presence of the 5th Dimension. As it has become named. It is the web of the gaps...)

I gave up films after five years, realising they could never give me the gift of avoiding the prison house of reason. There were films I could use as therapy and self revelation. But I could not MAKE such films. I walked away. Until the TER film...

Only in the desert and with my falcons, did I ever become at one with – face to face with – the godhead. That gnostic union with something "more"... and to discover it is MORE in every sense. I became the desert, I became a falcon... I became a Peregrine... der Wanderfalke... the Pilgrim Hawk.

The falcon is a pilgrim traversing the desert... pelerinage… looking for the tomb of the absent long lost father... call him Christ or God? I don't give (him) a name.

I accept that people can and do experience such moments of apparent (a -parent??) illumination... such as poets celebrated with their poems... and it is achievable through one form of trance or another... trance-ascendence... the dervish dance... meditation... etc etc... shamanism… as you know.

But these are NOT something I can attach to my experiences of film – by others or myself.

I saw Sister Carrie when it first came out. When I was 13 I think. Around then. Alone in the Granada cinema, half a mile from the slum I lived in with my mother. I walked there alone through the night streets. My father had just died. I had been picked to go "away" to a big big posh school... It was the film the Americans were showing that week in their Granada chain – that they owned. You had no other choice. The means of production and the distribution.

I went to the pictures once in a while. Alone always. At that age I knew nothing of what the film was to be about. I came out of the film – weeping uncontrollably – unconsolably... that final scene of HIM, the father, now a tramp... at the stage door... she gives him some petty cash... he leaves... "Don't leave, wait for me, please come back, see me after the show!"... But he leaves.

So who had been (for me) destroyed in this film? My father? Surely not. Me? Surely not. What had this to do with Isis and Osiris... and Horus?

I still don't know. I never read the novel. (She arrives... the girl on the train?) Perhaps I had simply fallen in love with Jennifer Jones... But I wept off and on for weeks and weeks. I had terrible nightmares... Something embedded, occulted in there... was it my future? Or my past? Was it a moment of being outside of linear time? Did I become vertical... vertigo... That is what Kamal Sahib would say and he was always right. He would say it was my future... my fate my destiny my story my myth... in a nutshell! And one day it would all come true and clear... he is dead now...

So – Orphée? How does it relate to Sister Carrie? It is about death and descending into the Underworld? Where I have lived ever since? La saison en enfer.

But it is about a poet (a failed one) who hears voices... voices from the R Field... in 50 years time I could write "The Risen"... I have always heard 'voices'. I do not need to pray... I merely listen to prayers being given to me! And the Warsaw Ghetto film? Why did that demolish me with the same savagery? A documentary film about the War and a Nazi photographer. And a young girl soon to die? A soul...

(All this is obliquely explained in my novel Nora and...) It has the similar mythic archetypal "story"...

The Ghetto as the Underworld... images often similar to those of Cocteau... it is the Underworld. It is HELL... on earth. But for the crux of my "possession" concerned the young girl digging in the mud... being watched and left to die. It was that DETACHMENT. Inhuman inability to identify... It was the inaction of the observer that hurt me so much... It would make me not want to be detached... and so I would become always in some ways a voyeur... as I would become a voyeur when I was sent to this huge school... this Institution... emotional ghetto of a kind... I was the odd one out... outsider always looking in... standing with my back to the wall... observing, recording... but this is too oblique. Me in Ashville, me in Columbia, me in the Warsaw Ghetto. If I felt myself always to be in some kind of ghetto – why? Perhaps... But why was it so devastating... this film... which came so much out of the blue...

Oedipus! His fate? Oedipus is a girl! He has a male persona and masks... but in truth he is a girl. He had no father to identify with to become male with and by and through. The Oedipal male is feminised from the start. His maleness is a mask... his true self is female. It was ME digging in the mud... in the gutter... as in my film Daddy, I was Mia Martin... NOT... not the phallic girl, Niki de St Phalle!

So in Sister Carrie... I was the actress... the young girl from the provinces in the big city... the world of theatres and movies! SHOW SHOW SHOW – business. Let me SHOW myself... my true self... no I will hide. Behind the camera... it worked for just a few years... until that didn't work for me!

As in my TER FILM... I am as much Maria Lenoir as Michael Schlieman?

Oedipus ends in a terrible trap. He has no experience of a loving tangible father. In fact he murdered him. (as I did!) He was from then on possessed and structured by the MOTHER... who he grows to hate – how can he escape that all-enveloping devouring Mother? He goes to the desert to be alone... over which the falcons hawks and vultures fly... in their circles etched on the violet skies...

In the desert... my eyes were finally open. As those of Tiresias – blind though he may seem to be, he has Insight that far exceeds mere sight... or Horus. I could see... "Voir pour voir et pas pour regarder." (Luc Dietrich). Friend of Lanza del Vasto... I wrote a treatment for a film once – called "Tiresias The Hooded Falcon." I wrote it for Bianca... she agreed to be in it – when we were together. Then I met Dido (her best friend) and we parted. Familiars... de Heimliche... la Blanche I called her... Mr Whitehead she always called me! (I used her voice in my film as you know.)

Do you know a book by Michel Butor – "Histoires Extraordinaires"... same title in an English publication. Very very rare. An analysis of a long letter that Baudelaire (Beau-de-l'eyre... from a good falcon nest)... wrote to a friend... about a dream. In which he visited a brothel. A dream? A visitation of course... great book. My bible.

WAR SAW... I saw the war... I see, I saw... see-saw... the Japanese pivot word...

I was always needing to SEE... incandescently... la raison ardente?... to see too much. That is Oedipus. Always afraid of going blind. Going mad... Watched (this young girl) by Tiresias who knows ALL! He who was initiated into The Mysteries... he who was once a sacred prostitute for seven years... like Salome... But his myth is against him – he must become blind. He borrows the eyes of his beloved daughter... Tiresias is blind but he knows the truth of all this. And reveals it to Oedipus... Eliot was trying to be Tiresias – and I think he achieved it. He had a very very powerful mother who wrote poetry and loved him very very deeply...

It is what Tiresias knows, in the play – that Oedipus does NOT know... that is the CONTENT of his archetypal drama... of course he needed to meet Freud and get psycho-analysed – or Jung – who would point out the same story crops up in all the myths where the father is killed... and the male son/ hero... like Christ... must take on the world alone. "Is it nothing to you... all you who walk by?"... Bach Cantata... or Steiner? I used to play that as one of my intros at school... with all my variations of course... a bit of Tosca thrown in... and La Traviata... I strayed from your letter and have no more energy.

I found the numinous in nature... very rarely in human artifice... and almost never in films. Which is why I gave them up. To LIVE the sacrificial... to become Le Pelerin... carrying their eggs thousands of miles on my stomach... and hatching them and bringing up the young falcons in my bedroom. ISIS of course... I never escaped her! Robin was a priestess of Isis... and in my novels Maria is an eco-terrorist – who murders her father! For killing Gaia... we never escape our myth. The private riddle each of us possesses, pursues us until our death.

I must go and make myself a Peppermint tea... an odd purple colour in a Temmoku cup...yes, resembling one of my favourite Japanese glazes... suggesting Lapis Lazuli... Eliot's "violet"... hour... a Blue Moon shining through the Aurora Borealis... "Behind the North Wind"...

peter

Re: (mo)Re: Joy
Tuesday, April 20, 2010 7:32 PM
From: "john sorensen"
To: "Peter Whitehead"

Dear Peter,

You write my thoughts – and, in doing so, you help me to think. I experience this with your latest letter, and I realize that it is something like what happened within me when I first viewed the film of 'Terrorism' back in February.

The sense of recognition is an important and dear thing, however it may arrive.

In reading your new letter, I feel encouraged to comprehend an idea that I have been feeling, but which had not yet been articulate in me: the sense that, in some way, 'Terrorism' is your first film.

You write: '(very important you realise I did not like ANY of my films – except The Fall – but I think I achieved something totally different with the TER film – finally – by accident).'

And in those parentheses you express something of my own feeling. There is, in 'Terrorism' (film), a special sense-of-accident in the beauty, which takes it to a place separate from (maybe above) the other films. This sense-of-accident is an important aspect of what I respond to in the work. (Or, perhaps, it is not so much the feeling that the beauty of the work is related to the accidental, as that it is an example of an artist being fully guided by their work rather than trying to guide it.)

In first knowing the new film, I was touched in several different ways, all at one time:

– firstly, by the raw experience of the film itself – the beauty of the images, the smokelike patterns of the story, the geometric interactions of the texts;

– also I was grateful for the way that the screen became a window on a story that was not on the screen… the story that begins to be more clear through the novels you share with me and through your letters and other films;

– finally, I was deeply touched by the 'way' of the film… perhaps by the implicit methods of its making.

For reasons related to those that are part of my love of Godard, I find myself loving 'Terrorism' (film) – delighting in the considered randomness of its structure and approach. It's like watching snowflakes as they fall and build up intriguing shapes on the ground where they land and amass. Even in their seeming accidentalness, it feels as if there is a logic or a pattern to them, but one can't easily discern what it may be. So it's best, maybe, to just let them fall.

I wonder about how the film was made: the working methods of the shooting, especially – which seem to me to be a part of the bigger story of the film. Was there a script in any traditional (or even in any Godardian) sense? Were the scenes developed through improvisation or through prepared dialogue? What of it is chance and what is preparation?

Through a series of happenstances, this morning I came to read a passage from a book by Evelyn Underhill. She writes:

'So, too, all who are sensitive to beauty know the almost agonising sense of revelation its sudden impact brings – the abrupt disclosure of the mountain summit, the wild cherry-tree in blossom, the crowning moment of a great concerto, witnessing to another beauty beyond sense. And again, any mature person looking back on their own past life, will be forced to recognise factors in that life, which cannot be attributed to heredity, environment, opportunity, personal initiative or mere chance. The contact which proved decisive, the path unexpectedly opened, the other path closed, the thing we felt compelled to say, the letter we felt compelled to write. It is as if a hidden directive power, personal, living, free, were working through circumstances and often against our intention or desire; pressing us in a certain direction, and moulding us to a certain design.

'All this, of course, is quite inexplicable from the materialistic standpoint. If it is true, it implies that beneath the surface of life, which generally contents us, there are unsuspected deeps and great spiritual forces which condition and control our small lives. Some people are, or become, sensitive to the pressure of these forces. The rest of us easily ignore the evidence for this whole realm of experience, just because it is hidden and interior; and we are so busy responding to obvious and outward things. But no psychology which fails to take account of it can claim to be complete. When we take it seriously, it surely suggests that we are essentially spiritual as well as natural creatures; and that therefore life in its fullness, the life which shall develop and use all our capacities and fulfil all our possibilities, must involve correspondence not only with our visible and ever-changing, but also with our invisible and unchanging environment.'

I think of what you write about 'That gnostic union with something "more"... and to discover it is MORE in every sense. I became the desert, I became a falcon... I became a Peregrine... der Wanderfalke... the Pilgrim Hawk.'

And I feel other things. Something in my single viewing of 'Terrorism (film)' touched on the nerve that Underhill exposes in the passage above. The tingling sensation has been sustained via moments in 'Terrorism (book)' and in the uncanny way that, again and again, your letters and books have taken thoughts or experiences from my mind and life and put them into words before I had mentioned them to you.

In a way, this is connected to my oldest responses to your work – from that time when I did not know your name, but only knew you in the shapes of the shadows of the work. For me, the beginning was in sound. Many years ago, I came across a bootleg record of excerpts from the soundtrack of 'Tonite let's all make love in london.' I loved the sound as much or more than I loved the music. From this 10" record, I knew the title of the film and I wondered at it. Only many years later did I come across segments of 'Tonite (film)' on the internet and feel again that shiver of premonition, which I still experience in moments throughout the other films, but mostly in the color or camera movements and captured scenes of 'Tonite' or in the child-gaze framings of moments in your record of the '14-hour technicolour dream' event or, perhaps in a more seemingly conscious way, in 'The Fall.'

You write, 'There is too much of the real (in a corrupted state) in a film/ed image – especially as it moves through time. It is never still...'

And I wonder: if this is true of film... then what about theater? What of the Mystery Plays? Are they 'unreal' enough – with stillness in them – to be holy?

Have you written plays besides the Kinski one, which you mentioned in an early letter? How do you feel about the play-in-film aspects of 'Benefit of the Doubt'? And in what ways may television (poor, bloated, undernourished TV) have a potential that touches on aspects of both theater and film, but with the power to go somewhere all its own... even if it hasn't yet? (Do you know of the early TV work of the American producer, Robert Herridge – his strange, confrontationally intimate settings of Dostoyevsky and his 'dramatic documents' of story-telling, music, poetry and camera movement?)

Thank you for taking me on the trip of your experiences with 'Sister Carrie' and the Warsaw Ghetto film and 'Orphee.' You help me to see how these things got 'in your eye' (maybe like a magic dust that doesn't blind, but provokes vision). I am curious to see 'Terrorism (film)' again, with these things in my mind's eye.

You approach difficult, simple, beautiful things in your letter:

'differing fragments of a single plot. My plot. My myth. My destiny... the story we inherit... being stripped of all previous "structures"... uprooted and plunged... with wide open scared seeking eyes...'

'BUT BUT BUT... I do believe in the numinous. There are no words to express it, so why should I try? let me just say...'

'I gave up films after five years, realising they could never give me the gift of avoiding the prison

house of reason. There were films I could use as therapy and self revelation. But I could not MAKE such films. I walked away. Until the TER film...'

I wonder: After walking away, how did you walk back? I don't ask 'why' – just 'how.' What were the stages on that journey, and is the trip still happening in some way?

I wonder if all of this may be connected with something else in your life about which I know very little: the illnesses (Reiter's syndrome?). I understand that you have encountered serious illness twice, both times during the process of making films. Is this true? What do those experiences have to do with those films – do they have anything to do with them?

You write, 'The falcon is a pilgrim traversing the desert... pelerinage... looking for the tomb of the absent long lost father... call him Christ or God? I don't give (him) a name.'

(In the Tao te ching, something like: 'The tao that can be named is not the real tao.')

You write about what affected you in your first seeing of 'Sister Carrie':

'I still don't know... Perhaps I had simply fallen in love with Jennifer Jones... But I wept off and on for weeks and weeks. I had terrible nightmares... Something embedded, occulted in there... was it my future? Or my past? Was it a moment of being outside of linear time? Did I become vertical... vertigo... That is what Kamal Sahib would say and he was always right. He would say it was my future... my fate my destiny my story my myth... in a nutshell! And one day it would all come true and clear...'

'I do not need to pray... I merely listen to prayers being given to me!'

'Oedipus is a girl! He has a male persona and masks... but in truth he is a girl... his true self is female. It was ME digging in the mud... in the gutter... So in Sister Carrie... I was the actress... the young girl from the provinces in the big city... the world of theatres and movies! SHOW SHOW SHOW – business. Let me SHOW myself... my true self... no I will hide. Behind the camera... it worked for just a few years... until that didn't work for me! As in my TER FILM... I am as much Maria Lenoir as Michael Schlieman... ?'

Once upon a time I read a Budhhist story, which I later forgot and which I now remember this way:

A monk was returning to his monastery after having been away for a long time. Midway on his journey he came to a small village where he decided to spend the night. He arrived late and the old widow inn-keeper arose to let him in and show him to his room.

During his sleep the monk dreamt that he was transformed into a woman – and the next morning he awoke to find that it was true. Not only had his body changed, but his voice had changed, too.

Due to bad weather that day, the monk could not leave the inn. At last he came downstairs to take breakfast. When the puzzled inn-keeper asked if her guest (who still wore man's clothes and had short hair) was a monk or a nun, the guest hesitantly replied that she was a nun.

The bad weather continued for several days. The nun knew that she could not continue her former journey as no one in the old monastery would recognize her and, in any case, there was no place for a woman back there. Instead she decided to stay as long as she could with the kind inn-keeper.

When the rains cleared away the inn-keeper grew afraid that the nun would depart. The older woman confessed that she had always longed for a daughter and that she would sorely miss her guest if she would leave now. The nun replied that she had nowhere to go and asked if she could stay for a time as the woman's adopted daughter. The older woman wept in joy.

The nun let her hair grow and the inn-keeper made several nice dresses that were appropriate for her to wear. Some months later the inn-keeper's son returned home from his travels. When first he set eyes upon the nun he seemed startled, but he soon composed himself and never again repeated this behavior in her presence. In time the nun and the inn-keeper's son fell in love and the two were married.

On their wedding night, the man told his bride that he had a secret.

What? she asked.

He answered: in his previous life he had been an unhappy woman who had brought much pain to a certain man, her lover. The nun's husband confessed that he had carried with him, into this life, feelings of deep remorse for his past behavior, and that he fostered a need to atone for his actions.

Why do you tell me all of this? asked his bride.

He replied, Because I believe that you are the man from my previous life, transformed into a woman, and I fear that you will treat me now as I treated you then.

The woman wept, for she now understood what had happened to her and why.

...Thank you for 'Histoire extraordinaire.' I was struck by this line in Baudelaire's letter about his dream:

'Then I reflect that modern stupidity and nonsense have their mysterious use, and that often what has been done for the worst, by a spiritual mechanism, turns out for the best.'

And by this line in your letter:

'...we never escape our myth. The private riddle each of us possesses, pursues us until our death.'

You write the phrase 'Behind the North Wind.' Is this a 'hello' to George MacDonald and his Diamond?

Yes, please send me a copy of 'The Risen' (preferably in a Violet Hour tea cup).

Peace,
j

being practical
Wednesday, April 21, 2010 7:30 PM
From: "Peter Whitehead"
To: "john sorensen"

Dear John

I am not very good at being practical these days – sorry to say. But I try...

I will answer your long email of two days or so ago, very soon. A lot to ponder and mull over...

Nature's Child – the novel. I have not dipped into it since I started the film, over three years ago – and abandoned it for Vienna – and the shift towards the first novel – towards the new title – Ter etc...

Last night I dipped into the text of the novel... and was amazed! It is so so very close to the film in a very weird way. And yet it is set in Cumbria... and we learn much about who the guy is, who gets murdered... and the narrative line is very different. But I know you will enjoy it. Weaves/waves in and out of the 'reality' of The Film – and the reality of itself! When I wrote it, I had never imagined there would be a film – and that someone might see the film and THEN read the novel – so the characters would be visible in the mind/space... I think it might surprise you. It surprised me.

Paul asked me to email him the texts of the novel – for you. I can't find the last version – only earlier ones, and don't have the psychic energy to go hunting. Just now.

BUT – anyway! – there is a much simpler solution. The novel is there already!!! Go to my nohzone website – address below – click click click til you reach the Nohzone tree – with the satellite websites. You will see there two lozenges... as I call them. One is ‘Nature’s Child’. Click. There you will find the complete novel! Divided neatly into chapters. All you need do is download it. Chapter by chapter. Or read it on line. Download and print is best surely. I think it is an easy and normal thing to do. There is also the FULL “Girl on the Train” novel... I dipped into that too. I have come to the conclusion that I am stark raving mad.

Triggered by these “dips” I have decided that I will persevere tracking through my thirty or so discs – to find the final version. It is only different in very small details. But it must be perfect. I shall make a final correction to the files... and immediately arrange for it to be printed as a book. Easy these days – even easier I am told in USA – with Lightning Source and the likes – “Print on Demand” printers seem to exist all over USA and are very cheap. Any info would be useful. Best to do it there – with Framework “opening” in New York.

BECAUSE I will publish the novel, as a companion to Novel One – to coincide with the Framework publication. If the price of doing that in USA is reasonable – it should be for 500 copies – cheapest paper – black and white cover – I might also do “Girl on the Train”. Then my trilogy is complete – it is done.

Because I see more and more that it really is one novel... each part morphing into the next... with the forth... as a two way plagiarism. Parallelism... as I called it as long ago as ‘The Sixties’ when I started writing novels.

I am exhausted. That's all for this evening...

Very best wishes...
Peter.

It is – it was – Robin's birthday on Saturday – so I am in a very very distressed state. Can't cope.

Re: being practical
Wednesday, April 21, 2010 10:16 PM
From: "john sorensen"
To: "Peter Whitehead"

Dear Peter,

Being practical is no virtue in my book, and I'm quite happy with any sort of unpracticalness that you may choose (or be chosen) to practice. I look forward to your thoughts on the latest e-mails, whenever and however they may happen to come.

I'm evermore eager to read 'Nature's Child' and your latest comments enhance my thirst. My only challenge with reading the novel via the website is that I don't have internet service at home. I go to the New York University Library to get on-line, so lengthy reading sessions are awkward – and print-outs are obscenely expensive at the library. I'll ask Paul if he could do a print-out for me. Let's hope for good things.

(I am happy to learn that you are stark raving mad. Welcome.)

It would be wonderful to have a book-print-version of 'Nature's Child,' and I hope that all goes well in your efforts to see this accomplished by the time of the Framework "opening" in New York. I grow curious to know if you will include any special images on the cover(s) of the book, or within. I don't know what I could do to help with this publication, but please tell me if there is something, and I'll try.

Finally, and most importantly, I am thrown back by the anguish of Robin's birthday and by the fierce struggle of that difficult anniversary. And I offer my love and prayers/meditations for her and for you and for all of nature's children.

Peace, Peace, Peace,
j

nature's child
Thursday, April 22, 2010 8:02 PM
From: "Peter Whitehead"
To: "john sorensen"

Hi there...

I have found a box file I did not know existed. 60 pages or more – a treatment, notes, and first screenplay of a film – based on Nature's Child! And called Nature's Child.

Written a year before I started filming in Wien. Very strange it is – based on the novel and yet... somewhat tangential. It has not been easy but I have finally found the original files on an old Windows 95 Computer. I will find a way to update the files.

However – very important you read the novel – if you still wish to do so – and I think you will be surprised by the differences to the film – and yet some core contexts (con-texts?!) are there – then I hope he/you watches the film for a second time. These mean early texts will then be more meaningful – as a means of showing how this film emerged as a film/novel – from a bunch of unfilmable novels!

best
peter

many things
Friday, April 23, 2010 10:00 AM
From: "john sorensen"
To: "Peter Whitehead"

p,

paul is printing a copy of the nohzone version of 'nature's child' (novel) for me, and i look forward to seeing the 'nature's child' early-screenplay, too. most of all, i'm longing to return to 'terrorism' (film) after a journey through these texts.

one of the great joys that i experience in godard is the way that his films and the processes of his films are so mysteriously and magnificently interwoven. i feel this, too, in some of the silent filmmakers. in the days when 'scripts' were more godardian: thoughts in the maker's mind or notes scribbled on the back of an envelope and developed like a dance with cast and crew. i feel something of this in 'terrorism' and hope that, in some way, we might share the story-of-the-story with the readers of the film journal.

other thoughts: for me, 'pierrot le fou' is a film by godard AND karina, as 'shanghai express' is a film by von sternberg AND dietrich. it is impossible to imagine the final work existing without the profound contributions of both partners. when i review 'terrorism' in my mind, i feel, more and more, the importance of the remarkable sophie strohmeier to the completed work. i feel that there is something in her spirit and personality that is essential to the film, and i wonder how her participation evolved and what you feel about her role(s) in the process.

peace,
j

everyday
Saturday, April 24, 2010 10:51 AM [Robin's Birthday]
From: "john sorensen"
To: "Peter Whitehead"

p,

everyday i am offering love and prayers for you and your dear ones.

today most of all.

peace,
j

NOH

Monday, April 26, 2010 8:00 AM
From: "Paul Cronin"
To: "sorensen"

john you need to find the buddhist Noh play PINING WIND which plw suggests you might want to take a look at. but then you probably knew this already.

25 April 2010

Dear John,

It is easier for me to type such a letter on the computer, rather than as an email. Herewith my first reply to your two previous emails.

Firstly, though – a general comment about progress so far on these exchanges of ours – at your request. I have no real idea how you will find some coherence in them all, but that is your problem!

We started by talking only about the TER FILM. (TF!) But soon it became evident that a perusal of the novel might be useful. Already you are reading "Nature's Child" – and I am sure you will feel compelled to read "Girl on the Train" – which is much much much more your novel!

The point is – these three novels are one novel. In three parts. The Nohzone Trilogy. None makes sense (if they ever do – or if sense was what was being sought) – without the other.

But I think it worth pointing out that it would have been lax anyway merely to talk of the film, in isolation, however strong the reaction to it as a film might have been. To reveal it critically – which is the task you have taken on – you surely have to ask: Why so many words? Why is it so weird? Why is so much left out? So much Dark Matter(!)? Can the film stand alone? Etc.

Perhaps my way of making this film was influenced, deep down – as I was doing a kind of Godard with it – was permeated by hauntings... unconscious perceptions and ideas that I picked up while doing the two Godard screenplays. Alphaville and Pierrot Le Fou. To sit in an editing room with a 35mm editing machine, for three weeks at a time... and the film in huge 35mm cans... and to go through it scene by scene by scene... DESCRIBING THE ACTION – (and what an occult process that is surely) – assuming (arrogantly) that it was possible to create, on and from the page, the means by which a reader might imagine the montage of images that were the finished films.

Preposterous. Firstly you have to have seen the stills – to see what Anna Karina looks like! To see her amazing black and white outfits? And Eddie Constantine!? All pretentious in a way, this process – but a necessary compromise. If you make a book that is to be the screenplay of any film – you have to do it in a certain way. Bergman was always refusing to allow screenplays! Had tight control over PERSONA! And the way Godard made these two films, and more – was NOT from a screenplay. As in mine, much was improvised. (Especially Masculine-Feminine).

Though I was intrigued to publish his treatment of Alphaville, because it resembled the film quite a lot. He said it was the only time he had written such a treatment – without which he would not have been given the cash to make the film, by a somewhat naive producer who'd not made a film before.

So what about TF? There was certainly never a screenplay. There were notes for a structure, time and time again – always wildly different, each time, as external circumstances changed and I was undermined: by "documentary" reality. It was, after all, mostly a documentary film – with fictional overtones, or undertones. Let's say – Harmonics.

Certainly a unique and dangerous way to make a film. That I would NOT recommend to anyone.

So back to TF and the Nohzone Trilogy of Novels. No-one could be expected to read all three novels first, and then see the film! Unlikely. The Trilogy of novels is, though, an Internet Novel... not three bound physical books. (Although I will do them as books also for people who hate reading from the Internet. Like me. I never did it once. Impossible idea.)

What I think we have – you have – is a project that is really, now, not merely to a look at the film – and think twice – but a further look at the three novels that were, very mysteriously, the sources of 90%, probably, of the 'content and/or ambience – the zeitgeist of the film.' What is unique, and, I feel – the REAL project to be squeezed out of all this chaos – is what is so rarely seen. The painful gestation... the pregnancy. Horus is after all the son of Isis – and his father is dead!!!! It's called Womb-envy...

Most films are made, cut and dried, and shown. A few bits leaked for promotion. Then came a few guys who made "Films of Films" – The Film in the Making thereof... Here is Marilyn getting her words, in her last film, wrong; and crying...

What I have always done – in my novels (not in my films until now, to this extent) – I have been a kind of spectator of the process; never not being self-reflective – always mystified by the process by which something is pushed along (against unforeseen odds) and finally achieved. Hard enough writing a novel... but with a film like this – kerpow! I was a permanent victim – sacrificed at every attempt to move forward.

I finally decided NOT to even try to edit it into a whole, which could be shown in a movie theatre, and "read" by an audience.

Here is the truly painful bit... It was only because I got ROBIN – who knew the technology which I didn't know – to upload all the film into my computer – a new Mac (which I had never used) with an editing Program (I had never used – I had never edited a film on a computer in my life) – but it turned out to have been a subtle way of forcing myself to do it. She did so much work – so diligently. Hour after hour of Mini DV tapes. HD. After that I had no choice but to confront it.

By that time the novels were forgotten. It was me and the available material. It was me in the Labyrinth confronting the Minotaur – and his Pandora's boxes of films!

The idea that it is possible – to go through the 3 novels – and then maybe the fragments of screenplays and notes etc etc etc – lots of pages!! – and trace almost everything that eventually seeped into the film – and say this is a meaningful and useful process... to whom? Maybe students studying film. I am humbled at the thought of this project of yours. For me, I reflect on the making of this film and I start to get angina! It goes straight to the arteries in my heart and constricts them. Sometimes there is so much stress trying to recall these three years – that I have to move away. Go to the garage and dig my fingers in the clay (like Mahler dug his fingers into the soil and mud of his wooden working hut) – and throw pots. It is a kind of madness. This polarity. This schizophrenia... But as Ronald Laing said. "The only sane way to react to a world that has become totally schizo-phrenic – is to be schizophrenic. Try to resist it and you get torn apart."

Madness or not – a film did get made. Is it a record of madness? Or about the Dangerous Cultivation of Fear of Terrorism – by the Media – is that not what the film is really about? And I think in this sense, it stands on its own feet – thanks to so much experimentation going on these days with Youtube Facebook etc etc Anything goes! But you saw the hidden agendas in it... as a Surrealist film about "L'Amour Fou!"

But I said it before. I was drawing a lot of ideas from ELIOT's The Waste Land (Thanks to my time spent developing my now-aborted novel) – and felt more and more I could go as far into uncertainty, ambiguity, misinformation etc – as he had done. His poem was obscure and, frankly, a total mess! No wonder it took Ezra Pound to suggest cutting half of it out. Which ELIOT did! That is friendship. (Also shows how insecure he was after all...) He knew it was a mess. It was still a mess after he cut half of it out. And yet... it was only a mess if you expected Wordsworth. It was a new form of mental montage – of Consciousness. In that sense it was perfectly clear. It is how we think and feel…

And as my film developed in the editing process I soon abandoned – very happily – any real effort to make it all easily read, as a linear narrative. Eliot's poem was the first that totally EXPLOITED the idea of hypertext linking... as he said in his NOTES. (Except most of the History of English poems from Chaucer onwards!!!!!) – The whole poem, Eliot said, is "written" by Tiresias. He whose Domain is

Hades... the Underworld... Where Orpheus had to go to find Eurydice... Let us not forget however... that the Japanese have been writing HAIKU for the last thousand years and more, and NOH plays, which depend totally on you knowing the codes, what is absent and not said – the occulted previous poems and texts – or other forms of recorded dreams! – (as in all forms of religion) – the cryptic links to that COSMOS of Dark Matter – The Past, Other Poets, Other poems and plays... that become the twisting weaving matrices of the Collective Unconscious. The very purpose of Haiku is to break through, to escape the present, go into cyclic time and escape – what Wordsworth so aptly called – "The Prison House of Reason."

"A Robin Redbreast in a cage sends all heaven into a rage." Blake.

My film – as indeed and especially, also, my third novel... "Girl on the Train" – (I should have called my film "The Girl on the TRAM!") is more an expression of Consciousness – the way the Mind really works – poised as we are on the interface of Memory and Imagination... mocked by the pivot words... than about merely film-making. Or writing a bunch of weird Internet novels.

It seems to me it is this DOCUMENTATION – this parallel documentary Dossier (a book within a book) that you are creating – that will be so much more important than the film itself, and the three novels. For FRAMEWORK and other Media Buffs, surely it will be this tortured genesis, the metamorphoses, which might be the REAL story of this involute of created forms.

Written by a man who is dying, who is certain he is running out of time... he must work fast... off the cuff... before he dies. His heart only 1% away from Total heart failure according to the Extrusion tests...

A film about DEATH. Fernando... Samantha... Robin... and Michael Schlieman... even Matthew Sutherland... even Peter Whitehead...

Now to your question about the GIRLS. Sophie, Samantha, Nina and Yelizaveta Tsyzina-Whitehead! Nora... Robin Vote... Nadja...

Well yes... I am too tired tonight for that. A book in itself!!!??? I will send that in my next letter!

Best wishes...
Peter w.

pining wind & autumn rain
Monday, April 26, 2010 8:15 PM
From: "john sorensen"
To: "Peter Whitehead"

p,

thank you for your fresh letter. i'm breathing it in slowly and surely, and hope to respond in the next day or so.

in the meantime, i've found a copy of the noh play 'pining wind.' it's a beautiful and enigmatic thing. as the translator says in his introduction:

'Noh is a genuine "forest of symbols." Not only can one roam through the trees happily and at great length; one can also get lost. Or at least one can discover enchanted glades and lose track of the way home.'

...not unlike my happy experiences with your new film and the steady streams of novels that flow on every side.

peace,
j

a letter
Tuesday, April 27, 2010 2:49 PM
From: "john sorensen"
To: "Peter Whitehead"

Dear Peter,

Do you know the lovely and painful play 'Kagekiyo,' by Seami (Zeami)? A translation is included in Arthur Waley's 'The No Plays of Japan.'

Thank you for your beautiful letter, which brings many interesting new thoughts and threads into our evolving story-about-stories.

You write (about your many messages), 'I have no real idea how you will find some coherence in them all, but that is your problem!'

Thank you for this problem... though I don't think it is one. In any case, why does there have to be 'coherence' [1: systematic or logical connection or consistency; 2: integration of diverse elements, relationships, or values]? I'm happy with beauty, messy or neat.

Have I, as you say, taken on the task of revealing the film ('Terrorism' aka TF) critically? I hope not! I simply enjoy your film and would like to experience it as fully as possible – which is what I feel is happening through this on-going journey that is winding us through novels and noh plays and old films and, soon, back to the starting point of TF itself. The detours may be the destination. And if we take some good snapshots along the way, perhaps the resulting slide-show will be of interest and help to others who, for now, can't or won't take the full trip. So: 'critical revealing' – no. 'A Guide to the Labyrinth' (as von Sternberg originally intended to title his memoir) – I wouldn't mind.

I find great delight in the notes you offer as to how 'Perhaps my way of making this film was influenced, deep down – as I was doing a kind of Godard with it – was permeated by hauntings... unconscious perceptions and ideas that I picked up while doing the two Godard screenplays. Alphaville and Pierrot Le Fou.'

This is how your film feels to me, and this feeling gives the work a sense of creative heritage that I believe is an important part of its 'risky beauty.'

You point out, '...the way Godard made these two films, and more – was NOT from a screenplay. As in mine, much was improvised.'

I wonder about the relationship between preparation and improvisation in TF. You write that, while there was no script in a traditional sense, 'There were notes for a structure, time and time again – always wildly different, each time, as external circumstances changed and I was undermined: by "documentary" reality.'

Could you give me any samples of these notes and how they evolved from words to pictures?

For example, in a scene such as the final one with you and Sophie at the cafe – what was the process that brought this key passage to life? Did you have any of the spoken lines prepared in advance? Perhaps your own but not hers? Did you discuss her lines (or, more importantly, I think, her gestures and 'looks') with her in advance? Were you aware, while making the scene, that it would be fitted into the final film in the important place that it has claimed?

In films such as 'Masculin/Feminin' and 'Terrorism...' perhaps the process is the product in a more clear (and important) way than in most films. In the end, I love 'Masculin/Feminin' as much for the little Grove Press book of it (including the Maupassant stories upon which it is 'based' and many other bits and pieces that somehow seem to be important parts of the whole) as for the version on screen.

You write of how TF has 'fictional harmonics. Certainly a unique and dangerous way to make a film. That I would NOT recommend to anyone.'

Do you mean that the fictional aspects harmonize with the documentary aspects? or something else? In any case, I agree that this method is unique and dangerous, and I take your loud un-recommendation as the highest of possible recommendations.

In an hour or so, I'll be meeting Paul at the feet of the metal Gandhiji in Union Square, where he promises to bring me the two next 'chapters' in the Nohzone trilogy, and possibly other prizes. I'm looking forward to these things with much eagerness and joy. Thank you for the 'three novels that were, very mysteriously, the sources of 90%, probably, of the 'content and/or ambience – the zeitgeist of the film'.'

In your letter, you begin to articulate why, perhaps, I feel much closer to TF than to your other filmworks: the way that, in this film, for the first time 'to this extent,' you have found a way to be, at one and the same time, a clear participant and also 'a kind of spectator of the process; never not being self-reflective – always mystified by the process by which something is pushed along (against unforeseen odds) and finally achieved.'

I think of Flaubert's inevitable 'present everywhere and visible nowhere' – and I think of Hitchcock's very visible (if brief) cameos and, especially, of Orson Welles' radio work with the Mercury Theater of the Air, in which he would introduce the story, slip into one or more characters inside it, and then transform back into the roles of host/director (and pretending-to-be writer), giving a cue to the show's announcer to sell Campbell's soup.

Too, I think about the way you are visible all-over-the-place in TF but, thanks to the documentary uncontrollability of many aspects, may not always be present.

I am deeply moved – and strangely joyful – in discovering more about the part that Robin played in this film. Somehow her role was very clear even when it was utterly unknown. The overt knowing helps to make some kind of sense of things that were pleasing but hazy in my first viewing of TF. And taking this knowledge with me into the next viewing is bound to have an effect – though I have no idea of what sort.

Keeping your description of her participation in mind, I start to feel that Robin is moving in this film in a very 'everywhere present, nowhere visible' way. In any case, I feel a wonderfully pure feminine force in this work in a way that I don't feel in any of your other films... or, so far, in the novels, either. Hers is a very welcome vibration, no matter how quiet and small, no matter how loud and large.

I love, 'it was me and the available material. It was me in the Labyrinth confronting the Minotaur – and his Pandora's boxes of films!'

I agree with you that it doesn't seem to be a very interesting possibility, the prospect 'to go through the 3 novels – and then maybe the fragments of screenplays and notes etc etc etc... and trace almost everything that eventually seeped into the film...'

This would be pedantic and, like you, I'm doubtful as to the productive uses of the end-results of such a campaign. But, even if it's not worthwhile to catalog the contents of our mother's handbag, still it may be fun to pull out a few items at random and wonder what in the world they've been (or will be) used for. I favor the handbag-fishing adventure, which (I think) we're already having. No angina-inducing investigations. Just a little rummaging for fun and holy-profit.

Do you like 'L'amour fou'? I've never seen it. Is it something beautiful?

You write about 'NOH plays, which depend totally on you knowing the codes, what is absent and not said – the occulted previous poems and texts – or other forms of recorded dreams!'

I see what you mean, but I don't agree with the 'totally.'

When I read 'Pining Wind' or 'Kagekiyo,' I know that I do not really know what I am reading: that I'm getting lost in a temple that (because of my ignorance) seems like a wilderness to me. And yet, I love the experience. Is that wrong?

Maybe it's not 'enough,' but it certainly is something. Isn't it possible to sometimes see things more clearly with less information than with more?

So: I reject the task of trying to reveal TF critically, but I embrace warmly the possibility of building (with you in these letters), as you write, a 'parallel documentary Dossier (a book within a book)' related to the film and the novels (and the weather this afternoon and all). I don't know if it's important, but it certainly sounds like a good adventure: a fast, off-the-cuff – and very-much-alive – adventure.

(I look forward to your next letter '...about the GIRLS. Sophie, Samantha, Nina and Yelizaveta Tsyzina-Whitehead! Nora... Robin Vote... Nadja...')

Peace,
j

the girls
Tuesday, April 27, 2010 9:32 PM
From: "Peter Whitehead"
To: "john sorensen"

I will answer your new email very soon... sorry I am falling a bit behind... But the girls are important after all!

peter

27 April 2010

Dear John,

This is to continue the letter of yesterday – written on my computer.

The GIRLS: I have already said too much, but I suppose that by now, there is no looking back. I hesitate to talk about personal, loving relationships – achieved or not – it does seem something of a betrayal. Godard certainly "said it all" in his "Oval Portrait"... = Vivre Sa Vie. To use the image and person of your wife – your loved one – as an image and actress in a film – speaking words you have put into her mouth... is somehow tainted by the notion of prostitution. Which is why he made the film about prostitution. But of course he then went on to say a lot about the predicament of 'Woman.' And money... The film is about exploitation of the female image. He is questioning it and admitting to it – I surmise – because he loved Anna Karina. And so, he had doubts...

But over the years he would go on and on and on... 'exploiting' his actresses, in various forms. That is Cinema... A girl and a GUN... But not in the truly corrupting sense. They were, after all – actresses – being paid. But 'Hail Mary'... must surely be one of the most perplexing films of all time, in this respect... The sacred as sacrifice...

Bunuel, Fellini, Antonioni, Bergman, Skolimowski, Von Sternberg... etc etc Baudelaire would have had a lot of say about 'Dreaming about Brothels' if he had ever been transported into a modern movie theatre to see films by such a bevy of broken men!

I think the film 'Sister Carrie' worried me so much, even at that age, because it was clear she left him (the man once so rich) because he could no longer "keep" (sic) her... no money left... and she wanted to be an actress! Her success on the boards paralleled his degradation on the streets...

My TF film is clearly about Maria Lenoir. But by the time I was making it, I had completely forgotten the role she played in my nohzone novels.

I am already into an "involute" here (as de Quincey called such knots of entanglements)... because I started to make the film – with and for – my wife! My new wife of the time. Yelizaveta Tsyzina. No doubt about it. My age related to hers – she was 20 when I met her and 21 when I married her – was very similar to those of Jennifer Jones and Laurence Olivier! I met her at the first showing of my Retrospective, in London (where I also met Paul Cronin in the same half hour! He met her first and she was very rude to him!!) She was working for The Other Cinema! She was virtually an illegal immigrant from Kiev. But exceedingly intelligent, and I thought and hoped – potentially capable of being a very good actress. I was hooked. I sent her immediately for acting courses. She did very well...

So the film began as a collaboration between LIZA and myself. Based on the second nohzone novel 'Nature's Child'. In which there are two female roles. Maria Lenoir and Yoko, the Japanese girl. Two eco-terrorists planning an assassination; of the man who is finally assassinated in the film.

We started filming in the village hall of the village where I was living. But without Yoko. We were looking for a Yoko. Liza found me a friend from Kiev who looked Japanese! Not quite right. I was feeling my way at the time... not having made a film for forty years and using digital for the first time. (The only filming I had done – for fun – was to start a film with Peter Doherty; never to be completed. I gave the project to Robin my daughter. And it killed her.)

I shot several scenes, completely improvised, with Liza – which were essentially interrogations of her by Michael Schlieman, of MI6. She was suspected of being Maria Lenoir. (As in the novel). I thought the material was interesting and potentially useable. She was very natural. We did the filming in Cambridge.

She went off to Kiev where a theatre company had agreed to put on a play version of my novel "Nora and..." – she would play Nora. A play version I had written for Liza. She was perfect for the part. Half Jewish like Nora... and the right age. Rehearsals started while my Retro was shown in Vienna. So she could not be there.

Vienna... Where I met Samantha Berger. From Peru... who looked (for me) to be a perfect YOKO... LIZA is extremely intelligent and cultivated – philosophy, Jungian psychology, and the cinema especially. Her knowledge of modern cinema is staggering – apart from Anais Nin and Paris in the 30s...

Samantha was also terrifyingly lucid and penetrating about the cinema – but mostly she was a Marxist – she spoke and lived POLITICS. She was in the real sense a potential anarchist and/or assassin. She was a journalist for a Peruvian film magazine called GODARD. She was covering the Festival for them. She wrote an article about my films – I never saw it – especially THE FALL – which she thought was extremely powerful and important to her. In fact it sucked her into my life, my power. My new film.

She was also doing a PhD on Von Leukeren (I think that is his name) – Godard's favourite anarchist South American (?) film maker. At first it was fine – she read my novel "Nora and..." (I have a letter in which she 'talks' about it) – then she read the first 3 chapters of Natures Child.

I had to immediately change my tactics. Now I wanted to film in Vienna. Cumbria would have to be abandoned. I started to write a "script" in fragments, working with the di-verse (per-verse?) materials I had... YOKO... Vienna... and Maria Lenoir – who had now disappeared. (As in the novel.) I adapted this idea to making YOKO the link with this secret absent Maria Lenoir – a link she would not reveal. From this point on Maria Lenoir was going to HAVE TO BE either invisible, unreal, virtual... or whatever emerged. It would depend also on whether I could use LIZA now – in Vienna. She had joined a year's course on Jungian Psychology at Birkbeck College University College London. And was doing an acting course for a year. We were married and still very very close, but when I said I had to film in Vienna and had found YOKO, and described her... we both suspected the unsaid – there were difficult times ahead.

I had left Samantha finding me a flat for a year. She found one. I flew to Vienna, took it; and she moved into the spare bedroom. She left her boyfriend's flat where she had lived. But she was having a very difficult affair with someone extremely influential in Vienna Cinema Society. And government. Whom I cannot name. It was a torn situation! As you will see from our letters... we were "in love"... but it was a fraught, almost impossible situation. Unless you were playing in a Movie! I was prepared to bide my time... making the film was the priority. We were using each other, very elegantly and beautifully – accomplices to the full – I sent off her letters from Paris! – protecting ourselves and each other from the entanglements of "others"...

Suddenly I was taken to a concert of the All Girl Punk Rock Group called "Who Killed Bambi" – who sang in English – all of the songs were British or American. It had been suggested I might film the concert... I had agreed thinking it might be amusing, even fun! They were amazing! I filmed the entire 30 minute concert in a single take! The bass player was Nina Erber... the girl that everyone said was the most beautiful girl in Vienna. She also played in a smaller group called "Black Flash". Her boyfriend was the drummer...

I was shattered. What poise and cool beauty! I decided she had to be Maria Lenoir. So I had to tell the group I wanted to make a film of them! – so I could get closer to Nina. I filmed other concerts... until I asked Nina if she would be Maria in my film. Immediately she agreed... (wait for this!)... her favourite movie director had always been Godard... she had seen Masculin/Feminin over twenty times she said – all his films over and over again. She had all my Lorrimer Godard screenplays! She knew whole scenes off by heart! Music? The Clash, Cocteau Twins, Durutti Column... etc etc... she was studying Eastern Philosophy and being Psycho-analysed at the Freud Museum. (Where I had been given permission to film over three nights, alone, in Freud's consulting room.)

Nina went there three times a week... she was painting strange pictures... and living in abject poverty. By choice... to be out of the system of money! I bought her an electric Cello – when she wept saying she had tried to learn the Violin as a child but her mother had stopped her!!!!!

She was Maria Lenoir... Was I going mad?

We started "going out" as they say – Secretly. It was difficult...

I was filming with Samantha... I told her that Nina of the Bambis might become Maria Lenoir... I got Samantha to help me to film a couple of the concerts I was filming for "My Bambi" film... (being made in parallel with the TF film of course.)

One night I had been filming late with Samantha. We went back to my flat. Two in the morning. Hungry. She said there was a Turkish kebab place she knew nearby – off she went. We ate two kebabs... and the next day she left to go to her University course. That night she was seeing her lover...

I woke up the following morning and collapsed... a full-blown attack of Reiter's Syndrome that had been in remission since 1968 when it had first attacked me. Normally you can't get it twice. The bacteria in the rotten Turkish meat was one of only three that can trigger Reiters. With a vengeance. When you get it a second time it can be fatal. "Instant Rheumatoid Arthritis". The pain is simply indescribable. I could not put my feet on the ground, couldn't sleep, couldn't eat, had permanent gastro-enteritis. Could not stop moving, the weight of my limbs and body were the source of the pain. I couldn't "put myself" anywhere to escape or alleviate the pain... it attacks the tendons where they join the bones. Arms ankles legs hips backbone... It attacks all the membranes... you just swell up and up...

I called Samantha. By the time she came to the flat I was lying on the floor barely conscious. (As she said later – she was sure I was dying before her eyes). I was... Draining away in every sense... I had not reached Samantha during the day – she was studying. I had called Nina. She said she would come later with some cooked food... She arrived at my flat five minutes after Samantha... with me lying in the bed. On the verge of losing consciousness – or dying... I wasn't sure... All this on top of the fact that I had chronic heart failure – it can kill you anyway. Nina wanted to take me to hospital. She had a friend who was a doctor... but I said NO! She said I was crazy. Instinctively... I knew I had to get back to England. I could not end up in a Vienna hospital, at death's door. I had no money to pay. Too tempting a target!

I booked a flight the following lunch time. Nina said she could drive me to the airport. I said NO... what if there was a car crash on the motorway? I had to get the plane. I would take the fast-train from the town centre. She said she would drive me to the train terminal. Fine. She came to the flat and picked up Samantha and myself... in her boyfriend's car. At the terminal, Samantha insisted she went with me to the airport, and I agreed.

I went to kiss Nina on both cheeks, to say a polite goodbye and thank you – but, in front of the two witnesses, I just fell apart... she was holding me up. I was crying into her hair... kissing her face... she was saying – "Will you come back? Will I never see you again? The film? The Bambis?" I had no strength to hide my feelings... and hers. Samantha was staring at us... in pain.

On the train... Yoko... the girl on the train... was talking talking talking in a trance, on a trip... she was talking about Tiresias... The Waste Land... we had talked about that Violet Hour several times while filming... not able to give the camera the right drugs! – The Vision of Tiresias... which is the world seen through the eyes of Tiresias... we had been filming Rilke's Duino Elegies... we were both crying. I was in agony – despite having taken so many pain-killers I was on the verge of losing consciousness... nothing had worked.

Samantha stared painfully at me... "I had no idea you were so much in love with Nina!"

Weakly I said something like... "I didn't know it either, until this morning!" Which was true – the extent of my feelings for her.

I never saw Samantha again.

It took six months before the Reiter's lifted enough for me to function. I was lucky. On a second bout, 4 out of 5 people NEVER go into remission.

When I returned to Vienna, I was told that Samantha "had had a breakdown and gone back to Peru." I rang her old flat. The phone was cut. Gone. Emails had gone anyway. She had completely disappeared.

Nina and I met and did some filming. I told her she had NOW the responsibility of carrying the "narrative" of the film. "I am not an actress!" she said. "A musician"... She was right. She simply wasn't an actress. Because she didn't like to be – to expose herself. And she could not improvise – it was cruel to ask her – and if I wrote a script, it was even more impossible. Putting words into her mouth. (Like LIZA she would correct them ten times until they became meaningless!) She drifted away... drifted into being busy...

BUT... I had early on learnt of a strange 'coincidence.'

When I first met The Bambis at the concert I filmed... 4 pretty Austrian Girls who sang 70s Punk songs in English! The story was they had been formed by an English guy. A theatre guy who worked for the Opera House. He did performance plays and that kind of thing. Nina told me about it over dinner at the Freud Cafe... "We never told you, but that first concert you filmed, where you met us – was our last concert. Our England manager... had killed himself two weeks before the Viennale. His photograph was in the Catalogue – In Memoriam!" The only reason, she said, that they'd continued playing concerts was for me... because I'd said I would make a film of them! Take them into a studio and record them. Get them to write their own songs. I became their MANAGER! In his place... and make a new rock film!

A road movie... Concerts in Vienna, Berlin, Bratislava... Death in Vienna? Go to Vienna and Die! It is indeed a dark place. I had unconsciously chosen it for the right reasons.

A month before I completed the editing of the film, I had to get in touch with the actor who played Vogelstein – to get a signature. He told me in an email that Samantha had killed herself. Gone up to the top of the tallest building overlooking Vienna and thrown herself off. A month or so after I had left, so ill to go back to England.

When I later arrived back in Vienna – Nina avoided me. I decided later she might have blamed me for Samantha's death. She had shown signs early on of being very jealous of her. Nina had watched my film DADDY several times and said she found it very compelling, true, but disturbing... and she'd bought a copy of my book BABY DOLL off Amazon – and said my images were exactly like her paintings. And suddenly Samantha was dead... but could she ever, possibly, have thought that my falling in love with her – had caused Samantha to distance herself from me?

So I had lost my film...

But by chance, nearly a year later after I'd left, Sophie got in touch with me. I had met her at the Viennale. She had sent me a copy of a film she had made. It was very good. She rang me in Vienna – out of the blue. We met. She told me she worked every Saturday at The Third Man Museum. I went there! It was amazing... a perfect setting. The wheel! The top of the wheel and looking down... "the Cuckoo Clock"... the man who is dead but is not dead... And the woman who looked like Nina. Sophie's favourite actress!!!!!! Who she was writing a long essay about for her studies.

I invited her to be in my film... "To play whom?" This time I decided not to risk anything. "Yourself!" I said. "But that is the only person I cannot play – and will never play!" It was true... very true. But we worked it out.

Which I will tell you about in my next letter.

Peter.

Re: the girls
Wednesday, April 28, 2010 10:27 AM
From: "john sorensen"
To: "Peter Whitehead"

p,

thank you for your letter on these important women.

thank you, as well, for sharing 'the risen' with me. it's a privilege for me to join you on this quest made of questions.

[looking up 'quest,' i find: 'a chivalrous enterprise... usually involving an adventurous journey' – and when i check 'chivalrous,' i find: 'marked by gracious courtesy and high-minded consideration especially to women.']

peace,
j

expeditioning
Thursday, April 29, 2010 10:54 AM
From: "john sorensen"
To: "Peter Whitehead"

Dear Peter,

Today I began reading 'Nature's Child,' and I have the strong feeling this morning of having re-joined an expedition-party from which I had taken temporary leave. I see from the thick map-of-pages on my table that there is a long way yet to travel, but I'm trying to not anticipate the topography or destination: to simply 'go.' In the meantime, I return to your newest letter, which gives me many answers and many questions. A few things:

You write of how, during work on TF, you had 'a full-blown attack of Reiter's Syndrome that had been in remission since 1968 when it had first attacked me.' Could you please tell me more about the '68 experience? Was this during the shooting of 'The Fall' (hmm, I've just noticed that this film could also be abbreviated as 'TF') – or did it occur during the post-production period? I wonder, also: do you feel that these two critical health emergencies were, in any way, connected with (triggered by) your creative work – or by the personal relationships that were such important parts of your life and work? Whether or not they were, I wonder what role your experiences of Reiter's Syndrome play in the finished films. Surely they had some kind of impact on the creative work, if only in adding a greater sense of mortality and lifting that solemn issue up to a higher place in the intentions/meanings of the films.

Concerning the Vienna experience with Reiter's, you say, 'Instinctively... I knew I had to get back to England.' What form did that instinct take? A simple sense that, for you, life was in England and death was in Vienna?

You write of the 'six months before the Reiter's lifted enough for me to function.' What happened in those six months? Were you able to work at all? Were you reading/watching/meditating? And how did those six months affect the work that you did when you returned to Vienna? When you watch TF (do you watch TF?), can you tell the difference between the pre-Reiter's footage and the post-Reiter's footage? As well, I wonder how much of the finished film comes from this pre-Sophie period of shooting.

I am very curious and eager to hear more of Sophie's involvement in the film.

Thank you for your kindness and beauty.

Peace,
j

unknowings
Sunday, May 2, 2010 5:15 PM
From: "john sorensen"
To: "Peter Whitehead"

Dear Peter,

I've just finished reading the manuscripts of 'Nature's Child' and of the various script-drafts that you sent via Paul, and... I have no idea what I think of them.

I am filled with unknowing, and all that I'm certain of on this sultry New York Sunday afternoon is that I'm grateful to you for the experience.

Peace,
j

Re: unknowings
Sunday, May 2, 2010 8:45 PM
From: "Peter Whitehead"
To: "john sorensen"

unknowings...
Dear John

I am sorry I didn't write to you these last few days. I told Paul to tell you I was really low... not able to function at all. Not able to communicate with anyone, while the depression lasted. Still not quite out of it...

Unknowings... What will we do if – imagine if you go back to the film after reading the two novels, and discover you don't like it now??

Perhaps it was unfortunate you saw the film and only then went to the novels. Perhaps it should have been the "right" way round, temporarily... Let us not forget that the order of their creation was – the three novels in the order as on the web. And THEN I made the film – something of a distillation of the three novels... after the event. (OOOpsss... I forget! In fact after writing the 4th novel – And Death Shall Have No Domain Name... which was itself a distillation of the 3 novels. A condensation... nice double meaning word?!)

I am starting to feel guilty – that you have been so unwittingly engulfed now with all these variations... and visitations of by my demons... Paul's fault after all. All I said after your first letters to me was a simple invitation – to you – to write a small piece about the film for my website!

DISSONANCE... Is the title of "Part Three of the Film"!! Multiple, cyclic entanglements – a deliberate Derridean deconstruction of logical rational linear narration. It is how we dream. And with dream we enter into the future... prepared to deal with it in the present. Rationality is a myth – the myth of the usefulness of measurement... le complot contre La Raison... is my film and my novels... La Raison Ardente as Apollinaire called it...

Yes yes, you say... unknowings... what is it you want to KNOW? Are my films and novels an invitation to know? Or an invitation to question knowing? Or an invitation to enjoy unknowingnesses... What did Keats say about the beauty of the pot? Perhaps the film is about the impossibility in this digitalised collective new zeitgeist virtual world consciousness, for us to be responsible for, or to, or able to KNOW, anything... in that old comfortable (self deluding) sense when people were sure they could know everything – because they could "take the measure of it" – just read The Bible! – and say Hail Mary a hundred times... (and whip the child who gives up at 66)... now, in this day and rage, what is knowing? Let Google and the Media do the work, and they will know it for us? We will take them "at their word(s)"... so much quicker, anyway, and we must be democratic and socially conscious so we must seek consensus and agree with every-one else who have already accepted what they have been given... By Google and Yahoo – (great words, no?)... for the new Gods... with their new prayer books... and creeds...

In the beginning was the Word... or... In the beginning was the Image? I say In the beginning was thc Drcam... and sincc so much has been lost – let us go back to questioning, challenging the true purpose and nature of DREAM... which is itself merely a preparation for the Imagination... In the beginning was the Imagination... we dream the questions, imagine the experiment, dare to try, go out and test it, and thus surrender to the mysteries of creating and comprehending a New universe... (Ooops, it just changed again, "go go go said the birds, man cannot bare too much reality")... for each and every one of us has a different universe. Each one – mine! – Unique and perplexing, but so so beautiful in its mysterious resonances and dissonances and entanglements...

The film and novels are not about knowing... they are about appearing to know, being arrogant enough to say – I know (qv Academia!!!!!!) – but surely we discover we/you don't know... that everything is in permanent flux, not even a probability of certainty, only uncertainty... every-thing and every person and every every thing... can be seen from so many contradictory angles. Especially DEATH... the greatest uncertainty of all. Unless you are lucky enough to be a Catholic or a Buddhist? Death... which haunts all my work. And betrayal. Dissonance – and betrayal. C'est moi! That is the only knowingness I have been almost certain of... betrayal... but you learn to live with it and play with it... The Rules of the Game – Le Regle du Jeu... what is The Game?... all this territory, these domains of my work – are they not treacherous indeed? Sorry... I never played with certainties... I preferred the Tarot pack! And the Egyptian Book of the Dead...

I daren't say it, but but... that "Girl on the Train" seemed to me at the time to be some kind of clarification. Of what had gone before. At least a kind of closure... But now that I think of it – probably not. Maybe it is just a stand-alone novel in its own right. I don’t know... I learned to live with uncertainty a long long time ago... in the 18th Dynasty??

Don’t worry if you feel I have gone too far into deconstruction of linearity... and you don’t approve. I more than under-stand! Or should I say – under-kneel? Maybe I should rename the whole Nohzone enterprise... “Schlieman’s Wake”? That wheeler dealer with words. I had a shot of MS, dead, in one of the Vienna Wheel carriages, alone. Maybe I should have used that after all. Rather than the tram?

best wishes
peter

in the beginning is the dream

Monday, May 3, 2010 10:35 AM
From: "john sorensen"
To: "Peter Whitehead"

p,

for me, the concept of 'unknowing' is nothing negative. i come to it through a 14th century text that i love: 'the cloud of unknowing':

'...And so I urge you, go after experience rather than knowledge. On account of pride, knowledge may often deceive you, but this gentle, loving affection will not deceive you. Knowledge tends to breed conceit, but love builds. Knowledge is full of labor, but love, full of rest.'

your books and films are offering me the opportunity of an important journey through confusion, into a direct awareness of 'unknowing,' and on to... what? where? of course, i don't know. maybe i can't know. but i feel that it can be someplace holy and loving, if only i persist in the correct spirit.

so far, i feel that i am persisting. joyfully. and i am filled with thanks to you for allowing me this trip: which is unfolding in what i believe is an ideal sequence of experiences and encounters.

i love your new 'in the beginning' words – but i prefer 'is' to 'was,' because, for me, the beginning always is. this is how i feel it.

in her introduction to 'the cloud of unknowing,' evelyn underhill quotes these lines from coventry patmore:

'Lovers put out the candles and draw the curtains when they wish to see the god and the goddess; and, in the higher communion, the night of thought is the light of perception.'

i am deeply sorry for the low that you have been in, and i am hoping (praying, actually) that soon you will feel better able to function and to live.

'the girl on the train' is waiting on my desk.

peace,
j

Fwd: How are you doing?
Friday, May 7, 2010 7:12 AM
From: "Peter Whitehead"
To: "john sorensen"

dear John

I have been silenced for the moment! Just can't break out of it. But I will – very soon, I am sure.

peace and eloquence to you...

peter

NYTimes.com: Max Palevsky, a Pioneer in Computers, Dies
Saturday, May 8, 2010 11:13 AM
From: "john sorensen"
To: "Peter Whitehead"

p,

mr. palevsky's story [see the attached obituary in today's NY times] is an interesting one. i was particularly struck by the final two paragraphs:

'Despite his groundbreaking work in the computer industry, Mr. Palevsky remained skeptical about the cultural influence of computer technology. In a catalog essay for an Arts and Crafts exhibition at the Los Angeles County Museum of Art in 2005, he lamented "the hypnotic quality of computer games, the substitution of a Google search for genuine inquiry, the instant messaging that has replaced social discourse."

'He meant it too. "I don't own a computer," he told The Los Angeles Times in 2008. "I don't own a cellphone, I don't own any electronics. I do own a radio."

peace,
j

pandaemonium
Saturday, May 8, 2010 3:02 PM
From: "john sorensen"
To: "Peter Whitehead"

Dear Peter,

Thank you for pointing me toward the tangled, painful beauty of 'Pandaemonium.' I was slow to find my way within it, but once I could feel the trail, the trip was magnificent: this journey to the capital of Hell.

On our tiny planet of timid films, it is something very fine to see a work that is not afraid to explore and even confuse itself: which succeeds because it doesn't mind sometimes failing (maybe even rejoices in its seeming mis-steps, like so much of Godard). The film veered weirdly at times... but somehow it kept finding its balance-point in a place of honest wonder. It fills my heart and head.

I am grateful (to Samuel and Dorothy and William, too), and I am wishing Joy to you.

Peace,
j

Re: pandaemonium
Saturday, May 8, 2010 7:17 PM
From: "Peter Whitehead"
To: "john sorensen"

dear John

I am still somewhat absent from myself... but always pleased to hear from you, with your provocative links.

yes indeed – so nice to read of Palevsky's ideas – and the life he led through them. Clearly – exactly what I have felt from The Fall through to my recent work. But... I have betrayed the cause somewhat – with four novels on the web, embedded within a whole virtual novel that encompasses them. Perhaps challenging the web's claims of certainty and truth?... But within the novels – and the TER Film, it seems to me that you have detected my dismay with the way the Net is enmeshing us. I wonder how clear that message is in my work. Probably not clear enough.

Alas alas... the "novel" I was fabricating with Robin – my Eliot project – was intended to be a complete demolition of the new zeitgeist (Can you demolish a zeitgeist, or merely hope to slowly erase it? Or its apparent Hegemony). Now that Robin is dead, I have no will whatsoever to enter any labyrinth that includes her. That project must die with her. That project will never be possible now.

Glad you found Pan's Daemon domains intriguing. I can't recall, at all, why we got to talk about it! I only watched it in the last year or so in relation to De Quincey and the Lake Poets... the setting, Cumbria, of my novels... which was clearly a counter-measure-weight to my underlying progress (subversion?) towards Japan, to the Japanese NOH zeitgeist I hoped to create with 'Girl on the Train'... which after all was the destination of the long long train and tram journeys... of the other novels. The final stop... the end of the line... dot.com

best wishes
peter

pilgrims & progress
Sunday, May 9, 2010 10:33 AM
From: "john sorensen"
To: "Peter Whitehead"

Dear Peter,

Thank you for your comments on Palevsky's ideas, and for affirming the link to your own thoughts – and to your feelings of having, perhaps, betrayed these ideals through your 'virtual' work.

Part of what interests me in your and Palevsky's journeys is that you both seem to be individuals whose natural (not 'artificial'!) curiosity leads you to explore all manner of possibilities: often bringing you to be among the first to investigate new ways of thinking and working and living. Such individuals are forever 'several steps ahead' of the masses of people, who follow in the explorers' paths (whether the masses know it or not). As well, the explorers are often also the first ones to reject the very paths that they have pioneered. To put it in an extreme way: few people are as strongly 'anti-alcohol' as is a former alcoholic, who has taken that trip from start to stop, and who has known the thrill of the experience and also experienced the terror of where that thrill can lead.

On the same day that the article on Palevsky appeared in the time, there was another interesting piece nearby:

http://www.nytimes.com/2010/05/07/arts/music/07sear.html?emc=eta1

...I was particularly struck by the lines:

'"There has been a serious deterioration in the quality of recorded sound since the 1960s, which continues to get worse to this day," Mr. Sear wrote in the late 1990s in a wide-ranging six-part critique of the music industry, "What Have They Done to My Art?," which is posted on Sear Sound's Web site, searsound.com.'

Curiosity and exploration are wonderful parts of human nature – but they may easily spin out of control, and can certainly bring the scientist and the artist to become pathetic examples of Wilde's famous 'Each man kills the thing he loves.'

Thankfully, there are those – perhaps Palevsky, Sear, and Whitehead among them – who truly learn something from their bold actions, and may be like old West scouts who come back to the wagon train to warn of dangers ahead and to suggest better ways of going. I don't know.

I don't think that zeitgeists can be destroyed, but certainly the 'spirits of the times' are always evolving, and each thing that lives is somehow part of that process of evolution.

In considering the term 'zeitgeist' I discover: 'The concept of Zeitgeist goes back to Johann Gottfried Herder and other German Romanticists such as Cornelius Jagdmann, but is best known in relation to Hegel's philosophy of history. In 1769 Herder wrote a critique of the work Genius seculi by the philologist Christian Adolph Klotz and introduced the word Zeitgeist into German as a translation of genius seculi (Latin: genius – "guardian spirit" and saeculi – "of the century").'

Perhaps our centuries have been marked more by terrible demonstrations of evil genius than by the movements of loving guardian spirits. But I believe in the love, and I feel that a crucial part of the artist's life and work is to be an instrument of that loving guardian spirit (St. Francis prays to/in the Spirit: 'Make me an instrument of Thy Peace: where there is hatred, let me sow love and where there is injury, let me sow pardon').

Have you ever heard the primitive 'singing computer' (1961) that was the source for Hal 9000's song in Kubrick's '2001'?:

http://www.youtube.com/watch?v=41U78QP8nBk

...I find it fascinating and disturbing.

Peace,
j

the birth of modesty blaise
Sunday, May 9, 2010 3:58 PM
From: "john sorensen"
To: "Peter Whitehead"

p,

perhaps you have noted the passing of peter o'donnell, creator of modesty blaise. i don't know much about his work, but i was interested today to read this story on the background of his primary character:

Mr. O'Donnell often said that the inspiration for Modesty Blaise came from his wartime experience. In 1942, as a sergeant in a signal detachment in northern Iran, he encountered a barefoot child in a rag dress.

"I told one of the guys to take a mess tin full of stew and a mug of tea to her, and when she got up to go, I'd put a couple of tins of food near her, so she could get them without coming too close to us, and a can opener, too," he recalled in a 1996 interview. "I surmised that she was a refugee from somewhere in the Balkans, and she had been on her own for some time, because she wasn't fazed, she was her own person, this little kid.

"And she washed the utensils in the stream, and brought them back to where we had put the tins of food, and indicated 'Were these for her?' We said yes, and she opened her bundle and put them in. She stood there for a few seconds, and then she gave us a smile, and you could have lit up a small village with that smile, and then she said something and walked off into the desert going south, and she was on her own. She walked like a little princess.

"I never forgot that child," he added. "I hope she is alive today; she would be in her 60s now. But when I wanted a background for Modesty Blaise, I knew that child was the story."

peace,
j

Re: pilgrims & progress
Sunday, May 9, 2010 7:10 PM
From: "Peter Whitehead"
To: "john sorensen"

dear John

Music: "There has been a serious deterioration in the quality of recorded sound since the 1960s, which continues to get worse to this day," Mr. Sear wrote in the late 1990s.

I spent the weekend doing music – sorting through the DADDY music for Mark Goodall (who is doing a piece in Framework about my music – from classical start, playing the organ as organist for the Ashville School for Methodist Ministers' Sons (!) – through rock n roll and inventing the pop promo – so they say – to the use in my TER FILM of post Tangerine Dream and Ashra and Popol Vuh Kraftwerk 'electronic' material...)

I have been playing my old tapes, 38 years old – recorded mono on a Nagra tape recorder – and they are still perfect. That broad analogue sound. Some very very weird stuff I did for my film DADDY... especially. Mark really likes THAT film. Really interesting how different people choose one to "privilege"... expressing their own personalities of course.

ZEITGEIST: This word has been disturbing me a lot recently. Hauntings are a serious problem at present. Freud and his Heimliche Familiars pounding in my ears. When I was in Vienna I bought a new Austrian book on Entanglement (they are doing some of the most advanced work on this subject there in Vienna) – hence my film! But it is also my most precious hunch in the present time... (zeitgeist one might say) – The Title of the book was “Einstein’s Spuk”... the cover appears in the film as I am actually buying it! SPUK? Yes indeed... But I asked what Spuk meant. “Er... ghost!” And therefore Z G should be meaning The Ghost of Time... in my reckoning... For Einstein it meant ‘action at a distance’ which he deplored. It has now happened. Events linked at a speed that is in excess of a million times the speed of light!!!!!

But I have been revealing my anxieties... at least to myself... I noticed that I was always spelling the word wrongly – zeitgeist... not sure why. And why have I been using the word too often recently. For the same reason I always buy clocks in Charity shops. Buying time? At least living in fear that I am running out of time... that time will soon no longer be haunting, or spooking, me... When time like a running grave tracks/hunts you down...

I would rewrite... When time like a running grave haunts you down.

I am a haunted man and on the run at the ‘present time’... which, even though it is “present”, it no longer has that certainty that the present should have. Giving presence... not even prescience these days... just the same dull dark death-in-life... deep deep uncertainty...

All my favourite pastimes embodied Robin... in the last six years or so since she came to me to discover who DADDY was and what it really meant... The familiar? The world at large... The superego at large? Or just mere ghost wearing a suit?

JS: Have you ever heard the primitive 'singing computer' (1961) that was the source for Hal 9000's song in Kubrick's '2001'?

PW: Loved it. It sounds very like some of the DADDY stuff I just found this weekend and not heard for forty years! well 38! I worked on EDSAC 2 for Francis Crick when I was at Cambridge... the second large computer ever designed and working in the Cavendish Lab for the MRC. I was feeding it with ticker tape data... fascinated by the new concept of such a machine that could think so much faster than we can. Hence why I used some images of my work there in my film Perception of Life – and used electronic music created by the BBC Radiophonic Workshop (I think it was called) in the film.

My music for The Fall... was done on a Hammond Organ – which I had never played before, recorded at Olympic studios... the electronic stuff. But made to sound as if it was pure electronic. I still like that music and feel it was good in the film – in contrast to the dynamics of The NICE... and America America... by Bernstein, under their variations.

Peace, to you too
peter w.

Re: the birth of modesty blaise
Sunday, May 9, 2010 7:48 PM
From: "Peter Whitehead"
To: "john sorensen"

j,

Great film [Modesty Blaise]!!! I had a flirtation with Rosella Falk, when she was in London shooting the film. I think we met because I was filming The Grand Film Premiere... in Leicester Sq. – and drinks afterwards... I think the scene is in Tonite? No? If not, I have it somewhere. She invited me to stay with her afterwards in her flat in Milan. I didn't dare! I figured I might never get out.

The story of the "gypsy" girl is very touching indeed. I have a similar experience, which however, couldn't be more dissimilar!!!! Not real but imaginary. Virtual... until... When I was a kid – 12 + – I used to walk in the evening to the Prom Concerts at The Albert Hall in London – from our Council Tenement Flat in Wandsworth. Alone. I would go whenever I could through the summer. I was totally "into" classical music. One night I was listening to a tone poem by an English composer – whose name I forget (but a great guy I recall) – the poem called Tam O'Shanter. In the program was the tale of Tam... a poem (or Scottish legend) by Robert Burns.

Tam is fleeing... running away!!!! – sic – I don't recall what from... (but it sounds very much like me... my father had just died... the wanderer had been born...)... and in the woods he hears strange music. He is drawn by it towards a Gypsy encampment. He is very frightened, and knows he must keep hidden. He has seen a dancing girl in the centre of a ring of men. Whirling and whirling... (Shades here of Sacre du Printemps by Stravinsky, of course) – She is dancing wildly, in a very very short skirt... the savage pagan dance of an entranced Gypsy girl... whose name he hears shouted out... "Cutty Sark"!

Tam is sucked more and more into the ecstasy until he cannot control himself and stands up behind the circle of men, and shouts out – "Well Done Cutty Sark!" The girl stops... the men turn on Tam, aware their circle, their tribe, has been penetrated in their secret ritual in the dead of night... and Tam has to flee again, even more furiously, running for his life... chased by the band of angry men...

For years and years I kept a diary – for more than ten years I kept a diary after this event in which at the end of every entry, late at night, I would write – "Well Done Cutty Sark!" (Instead of "And so to bed!") One day I discovered there was a famous boat called "Cutty Sark" in Greenwich and went to visit it. It was the fastest sailing ship in the English Navy. It was given its name because of its Short Sails... whereas Cutty Sark – meant Short Skirts... in Gaelic.

In December 1972 I was in Regine's NIGHTCLUB in London – the most famous nightclub of the time – with several of my Arab Princes and their Algerian whores. (I never went to nightclubs – this was to keep them company!) I was there two nights. The first night I got drunk and danced with one of the whores, (the princes were too reticent) – and we danced everyone off the dance floor! The prince offered me the girl for a week! Being English I declined. The next night I was more subdued. I felt I'd made such an exhibition of myself. Suddenly I noticed four girls going onto the empty dance floor. They danced together very erotically... one was Black, two were English and the other one looked like a Gypsy to me... but never would you have seen a more Dykey group of girls dancing alone on a dance floor! I turned to Prince Fahad and said – "Fahad, see the girl in blue! That is the girl. That's the one!" "What do you mean?" he asked, clearly confused. "You will see! I want her!" He laughed. "Never never! They don't like men, can't you see it?"

I got up and walked into the dance-floor, watched by a gang of Arab Princes and God knows who else of our ruling Elite... I walked up to the group and danced, behind them, then edged in... edged the girl in blue out of the quaternio and edged her towards a corner. She never looked me in the face. I was staring her out, and she knew it. She was scared... We danced three dances and she said she must go. The other three girls were still dancing alone. I thanked her and asked her her name. She said "Dido..."

"But you are Bianca's friend!" I stammered out – astonished. I was "going out" with Bianca at the time! Many times she had said we must go out in an evening and meet Dido... "You will like her. She is just your type!" Dido said – "Yes of course... you must be Peter. Those are your Arab Falconers!?" We met for lunch the next day. She flew to Bhutan the next day. I went to Algeria and flew falcons for a month. I returned Jan 20th, moved her out of her mother's house that evening, and married her on the 28th. Bianca came to the wedding lunch...

Dido's mother was a Gypsy... her name was Jill Pretty! She was Christian Dior's favourite model in Paris at the time she met Dido's father. Mere coincidence of course...

best wishes
peter w.

tam o shanter

Monday, May 10, 2010 7:48 AM
From: "Peter Whitehead"
To: "john sorensen"

J

I missed out the most important bit!

The music builds up towards the climax when Tam stands up and shouts out – "Well Done Cutty Sark!"

And we hear the words being shouted out amidst the music… (but as I had read in the program notes…)… it is not a human voice! It is a trombone that "speaks/sings" out the words. For me it was a moment of extraordinary mystery and power… I was listening intently, waiting waiting to hear the words, not to miss the words… and suddenly they were there! I heard them!

And as you see, I never forgot it – and its influence was quite weird, to say the least…

p

well done, cutty spuk
Monday, May 10, 2010 12:26 PM
From: "john sorensen"
To: "Peter Whitehead"

Dear Peter,

Your letters are trips for me. Often difficult, but always wonderful. At times I feel as if I'm being led/flown blindfolded through a series of strange and interesting places, and that the blindfold is occasionally lifted up or taken off (or maybe just slips down) to grant me a glimpse of another intriguing scene – sometimes only in part, sometimes in whole – then the blindfold goes back on and I'm carried off to another scene, somewhere else in the mystic woods.

Well, that's how it seems, and I enjoy it very much.

I'm working on another project (a performance-piece with a friend: a soprano from Korea) concerning the creative relationship of Cathy Berberian and Luciano Berio. It's subtitled, 'The Muse as Creator and the Creator as Muse,' because it's so difficult at times to tell, in the relationship of B & B, who was being inspired and who was doing the inspiring. 'Sequenza III' is so clearly an expression of Berberian's very particular gifts and tastes that it seems odd to call it a composition by Berio alone. Another aspect of the project involves the work of B & B's friend John Cage (and his muse/creator relationship with Berberian and with Berio). Bruno Maderna is part of the story, as well. Berberian was a woman who seemed to achieve at the highest levels when she was involved in a 'creative menage a trois' with her husband and a third artist.

Do you still play/create music?

What was it about the idea of 'action at a distance' that Einstein found deplorable. Do you agree with him?

I have questions that may be none of my business to have answered, but I hope you don't mind if I ask them. I ask them in love and respect. You write, 'All my favourite pastimes embodied Robin... in the last six years or so since she came to me to discover who DADDY was and what it really meant...'

I feel that the reborn relationship you shared with Robin is an important part of your own work in this time: TF included. I wonder what are the lost pastimes to which you refer, and if you feel that your time with Robin was part of your journey back to film.

Perhaps the reason I am thinking of the Berberian/Berio project today is because it seems to me that there is also an aspect of the 'muse as creator/creator as muse' experience in your own life and work. I don't know.

Could you tell me more about how the music for TF was prepared and how it was integrated into the film?

The Berberian/Berio work also deals with the experimental days at RAI, including various adventures in the compositional uses of recording tape and texts and such. Do you care for Cage's 'Fontana Mix'?

Your notes on the music for 'The Fall' remind me that one of my favorite moments in the film is the beautiful way that you place P.P. Arnold's lovely song over the top of the 'Eat, Drink and be Merry for Tomorrow etc.' party at Columbia not long before the police come calling to say 'goodnight and amen.' Whenever I see that scene, I wonder what music was actually playing at that party, before you added Ms. Arnold to the mix, and how did the change in music change the feel of the scene?

Have you seen the Guido Crepax book called 'Laterna Magica'? I think it may be the apotheosis of the Valentina series: pure silent cinema, in which the entire odyssey of the story is told/shown without a single word of dialogue. I like it very much.

Thank you for your tale of 'Tam O'Shanter.' I'm curious to hear the music that you heard. In trying to figure out who was the composer, I discover the 'Tam O'Shanter' overture by Malcolm Arnold is from 1955. There is also a symphonic ballad of that name by George Whitefield Chadwick from an earlier time – but he was American, not English. Are either of these the music that you remember?

Thank you for the story of your meeting-dance with Dido. But I wonder: can any coincidence truly be 'mere'? Do you know the story that Christopher Isherwood used to tell about the backstage meeting of Sarah Bernhardt and Swami Vivekananda? He ends the tale by saying something like, 'In the end, we have no idea how the meeting came about or why – or what these two remarkable human beings discussed or did. All we can know for certain is that it was no accident.'

Thank you, most of all, for hearing voices in trombones, o thou Pierre d'Arc.

Peace & Peace & Peace,
j

Re: well done, cutty spuk
Tuesday, May 11, 2010 7:37 PM
From: "Peter Whitehead"
To: "john sorensen"

sorry for delays... still below the threshold...

– I play the guitar – trying to evolve a new kind of music. Nothing on keyboards. Just electric guitar – synth.

JS: What was it about the idea of 'action at a distance' that Einstein found deplorable (or 'spuky'?)

PW: Einstein called it his caput nili... I think. That no actions could influence another across a vacuum. But qv Google.

JS: I feel that the reborn relationship you shared with Robin is an important part of your own work in this time: TF included. I wonder what are the lost pastimes to which you refer, and if you feel that your time with Robin was part of your journey back to film.

PW: Don't ever want to talk about Robin – from now on.

JS: Could you tell me more about how the music for TF was prepared and how it was integrated into the film?

PW: All the music for TF was composed in Saudi Arabia in a studio I built there while breeding falcons... I have fifty hours of it at least. All of it is improvised... I used two lots for two films for Arabia TV. I have one as a CD. Called "Desert Music" if you want to listen to it. So NOTHING in the TF music was related to the film in any way at all. It was made in the 1980s on a few synthesisers...

JS: Thank you for the story of your meeting-dance with Dido. But I wonder: can any coincidence truly be 'mere'? Do you know the story that Christopher Isherwood used to tell about the backstage meeting of Sarah Bernhardt and Swami Vivekananda? He ends the tale by saying something like, 'In the end, we have no idea how the meeting came about or why – or what these two remarkable human beings discussed or did. All we can know for certain is that it was no accident.'

PW: Romantics never see coincidence as accidental. I call it The R Field... which exists. As Jung knew... Synchronicity... my work in Pakistan convinced me of the 'fifth dimension' – forever! I decided later it was Holographic. As in THE RISEN...

JS: Thank you, most of all, for hearing voices in trombones, o thou Pierre d'arc.

PW: Are you Jean D'ARC then?

pw

Re: many thanks
Tuesday, May 11, 2010 7:40 PM
From: "Peter Whitehead"
To: "john sorensen"

John

I will send you a full account of "Sophie" – remarkable as you say – one day soon. I think the film itself – and some comments from me about Sophie – and the texts of sms messages – and the narration... is/are more than enough for any article on the FILM!

I watched the film tonight. There is not a single image or zoom or word or musical phrase that is not linked... like pivot words... backwards and forwards. It really is a poem – rather than a film. In the old sense of film.

But all that's up to you.

pw

Re: Glacier park turns 100, but age has not been kind
Wednesday, May 12, 2010 10:59 AM
From: "Peter Whitehead"
To: john sorensen

Thank you for this... [NY Times article re: Glacier Park] We are of course mad. Cumbria had the worst ever floods this year... And I am sure the Snow Country this winter will disappear under 25 feet of snow rather than ten... And now Montana ceases to be a lucrative tourist attraction for fear of being washed away into the polluted dying rivers and dead seas...

Yes, we are mad. What went wrong? Will prayers solve the problem? Will they convince enough people to ACT... become anarchists and confront the "powers that be"... as Marx always said, alas... religion has failed us utterly. Will science save us?

best wishes
peter w

thresholds, mysteries, dreams
Wednesday, May 12, 2010 11:22 AM
From: "john sorensen"
To: "Peter Whitehead"

Dear Peter,

I agree that TF is a poem rather than a film (in the 'old sense'). That's why I love it more. For me, the full experience of TF (which, in some way, includes the novels and the glow of the other beauties that I am being allowed to see and hear and read – from 'The Pining Wind' to 'Pandaemonium' to 'Hexagrams' to 'Snow Country' and this correspondence, too) is a Mystery that feels (so far as I am able to feel and guess) a little Eleusinian – whether like the greater mysteries or the lesser ones, I am too small to say.

And yet I keep on talking.

Peace,
j

p.s. I am Jean D'arc in the evening and Jean L'ight in the morning. Except when I'm not.

Re: Glacier park turns 100, but age has not been kind
Wednesday, May 12, 2010 11:48 AM
From: "john sorensen"
To: "Peter Whitehead"

p,

isn't 'science' a religion, too – another thing with a name that is not really anything? "The tao that can be told is not the eternal Tao/The name that can be named is not the eternal Name."

martin buber: 'I don't like the word "religion." It has become a foxhole through which the fox escapes just when you thought you'd caught him and he couldn't get away this time.'

religion and science are, in my mind, toys and tools (words, words, words) – things that kill as easily as they amuse or aid.

love isn't a toy or a tool. i think that it's something more. i feel it's all that is.

well, this is just what i believe.

peace,
j

NYTimes.com: Godard, With That Certain Je Ne Sais Quoi at the Cannes Film Festival
Tuesday, May 18, 2010 9:58 AM
From: "john sorensen"
To: "Peter Whitehead"

[LINK: Jean-Luc Godard has a new work, "Film Socialism," but he mysteriously doesn't appear at a press event at Cannes.]

Re: NYTimes.com: Godard, With That Certain Je Ne Sais Quoi

Tuesday, May 18, 2010 8:05 PM
From: "Peter Whitehead"
To: "john sorensen"

dear John... Jean...

Thanks for this link – but it has decimated me! Two red headed parrots on a tree? Qv the epigraph of The Risen – and second image on my nohzone website!!!

Paul also sent me a Godard interview about his new film that has demolished me even more. I am shattered. It is an interview between Daniel Cohn Bendit and Godard. I see there was a link in the piece YOU sent to me – to this interview. Nicole Brenez sent me a link some time ago to the trailer for the film.

But the use by him of fragments of sub-titles – many languages etc???? Do you really need much more now – for your piece on my film?

I have been low low low... so not finding words easy. BUT BUT... I am drawing closer to the most important "letter" I will send you – which I think ought to focus much of what my film is about. I will write it as a short text-essay and send it as an attachment. A useful exercise for me. The "story" of how Sophie came into it (drifted in sideways) and how the film became "A dialogue between Peter Whitehead." The subtitle to the press PR that I insisted was published for the Festival showing in Vienna. I do have many more "interviews" with her that were not used in the film. Useful for a DVD I think.

best wishes
peter w.

Re: NYTimes.com: Godard, With That Certain Je Ne Sais Quoi
Wednesday, May 19, 2010 10:01 AM
From: "john sorensen"
To: "Peter Whitehead"

Mon cher Pierre,

I'm sorry that the latest link decimated you and i hope that you will soon be... what? re-cimated? In any case, I hope for good things for you, now and ever.

I will be disappearing for the next week or so, as my parents are coming to visit me tomorrow and we'll be driving up to the Boston area. I will have limited e-mail access over the course of the next 10 days, but I look forward to soon reading the story of Sophie's 'sideways drifting' into TF... and whatever other thoughts and wonders may come up along the way. I feel sure that this marvelous document will be a key element in our discussion/exploration of your poem-film.

Even if I am not able to write to you over the next week, please know that you are ever in my thoughts and meditations, and that I am sending you my very best good vibrations of love – and peace and peace and...

Peace,
j

sense and madness

Friday, July 2, 2010 2:14 PM
From: "john sorensen"
To: "Peter Whitehead"

Dear Peter,

You are very much in my thoughts and meditations. Every single day I am wishing you good things.

I will soon begin re-reading our past letters (all 133-so-far print-out pages of them!) – to better remember where our dialog has already gone and to try to understand what route it might best take as it makes its way to nest in the journal that Paul is editing.

I'm hopeful that my re-reading may also provide a good opportunity to begin the editing process... seeing if there is a natural shape to the shared thoughts of the letters and, if so, how it may be clarified and revealed for any future readers that may come its way.

Other things:

I have had a strange, powerful experience with your trilogy of novels. I read all three books with eagerness and curiosity, discovering within them many (amazing, upsetting, intriguing, beautiful, curious) things which, I feel, help me to have a better sense of your spirit and concerns. Weirdly enough, when I was only 15 pages from the completion of my journey through the trilogy – in the final pages of the final book – I had the strongest feeling that I should stop, right where I was, and not go any further at that time. I have no explanation for this feeling, but somehow I sensed that it was wise to obey it. Perhaps there is something in those final pages that I'm just not ready for at present, I don't know.

I'm eager to watch "Terrorism..." again, but I am holding off on that experience until I feel we have more-or-less completed our dialog (including 'Sophie's Story') about the film. Then, with the ideas and lessons of our exchanges in mind, I'll be most curious to see how the film seems to me when seen from 'the other side' of my odyssey of reading your messages and comments, as well as the trilogy of novels (at least all except those mysteriously abstained-from 15 pages), having screened almost all of your previous film and video work, and even having had the privilege of hearing some of your music.

Today, when thinking of "Terrorism..." I have the strong sense that it is your most successful work. I am still haunted by the beauty of stray images from the train and, perhaps most especially, by the presence of Sophie.

As I've suggested in earlier letters, one reason I believe "Terrorism..." is the best of your films is that I feel it is less 'isolationist' than your other work. It feels like a healthy and true collaboration, combining your own potent gifts and abilities with those of Sophie and, perhaps, of Robin, too.

Film is (as the cliché, more-or-less truthfully, goes) a collaborative medium. And yet almost all of your earlier film works were individualist to a stunning degree. For my taste, your work is greatly enhanced – and at its best – when other spirits and voices are clearly involved in the creation. This is what I enjoy, in a related way, in my other favorites of your work: 'Wholly Communion' (which is a kind of collaboration-by-necessity with Ginsberg, the other poets and even with the Albert Hall) and that part of 'The Fall' which is, for me, a de facto collaboration of yourself with the students inside Columbia and a particular, remarkable moment in time.

When a single artist is the producer, director, writer, cameraperson, editor (and, sometimes, even the on-camera subject) of a film, things can begin to feel disturbingly claustrophobic... as if the person is producing a child by means of self-mating. I don't say that it's impossible for such self-based work to succeed, but it seems to be a perilous mission.

For me, for the most part, the stronger the spirit of the author, the greater the need for balance through strong collaborators. I find Godard to be at his best when he has Coutard and Karina to add their genes to the pool of the film that is being born.

In first watching "Terrorism..." I was not overtly conscious of why or how the film was working for me – it simply touched me, shook me, and that was enough. Now, looking back and considering our many messages and letters and my studies of your life and work, I feel more and more that "Terrorism..." works so well because in this film more than any of your others, there is a sense of companionship and collaboration: that, in "Terrorism...", other able spirits are at work, mixing their contributions with your own in ways that spur you on to do better and better work of your own.

Does any of this make sense, or have I gone mad along the road? Or both? I'm curious to hear your thoughts.

Love,

j

Re: sophie
Thursday, July 8, 2010 6:03 PM
From: "Peter Whitehead"
To: "john sorensen"

[Message contains attachments1 File (34KB) peterwhiteheadandme.docdear]

john... in haste

Sophie promises to do the second draft very soon. ten days at most. As she is on holiday this seems fair. It will be a tightening up of draft one – but with many more links to films and subjects we spoke about during our film sessions – books, opera, politics and so on.

Meanwhile she says you can read the very loose first draft – herewith attached. To get the flavour.

I am replying to your email and its questions – in my head! I will do it soon – together with more comments from me on Sophie.

Meanwhile I suffer with you – editing so many chaotic fragments!!!!

best wishes
peter (under pressure)

[Sophie's Story – draft #1]

As with most things that cling to our memory, there were a series of circumstances leading up to my first encounter with Peter Whitehead. I was eighteen then, obsessive, fragile, and bursting with opinions and awe. One of the highlights of my year would be the Viennale film festival I loved so much I would sneak into the press conferences just to increase my delight in expectance. There, Hans Hurch said something about Peter Whitehead. I probably wasn't listening but I jotted down the name and bought one ticket for Tonite Let's All Make Love in London, because I had no idea what I'd see and that's what film festivals are all about.

The night of the screening I remember was rainy and dark, or at least cold, and I'd just come back from a violin lesson and was tired and hungry and just wanted to get home but I knew I'd regret missing the film and the Q&A afterwards so I went, carrying my violin on my back.

Peter's appearance onstage after the film didn't surprise me at all. He came, and joked, and I didn't laugh, and then he said, "Film is fascism, it is a rape of the senses."

And of course I had never heard a film maker say that before, but I'd grown up in a world so anti-TV, anti-film, anti-image that all my life I'd been busy justifying my love for the cinema. I was irked. Peter continued: "If I say to you, 'A woman walks into a room with a blue dress...' you will all see a different woman in your heads. If, in a film, a woman walks into a room wearing a blue dress, you all see the same thing." Yes, yes, yes. That was so odd, that. I put up my hand. "If we see a woman wearing a blue dress in a film, doesn't she evoke a different something in everybody watching?"

Peter did this movement with his hand. "That's something else," he said. He went on. I forget about what, because he had mentioned a woman walking into a room wearing a blue dress. That was such a lovely image, that, and I still like thinking about it. We never actually finished this argument; I'm going to have to bring it up sometime.

But Peter and I, a few minutes later, ended up discussing books. He asked me to come around later so he could tell me what else to read. We kept on talking after that. We'd meet and we'd talk. I know now that what I found fascinating then encompassed about the tiniest fraction of what he found fascinating – but I suppose he enjoyed discussing those things anyway. We talked about the films, books, operas we loved; we talked about politics, and mermaids, and nightingales, and myths, and ghosts, and the romantics, and stories, and women mostly, and so on, everything I'd always wanted to talk about to someone but, being the sheltered gauche 18-year-old, for lack of people, never could.

At some point right at the beginning, Peter mentioned the film he was making, Terrorism Considered as One of the Fine Arts. *I remember thinking, "cool, maybe he'll let me help". He later did ask me to assist him. I was thrilled to bits to have a task in the world when I was supposed to be doing schoolwork.*

By the time Peter turned the camera on me we had already established our own world to which we were both the only accomplices. Actually, this is what might sum it all up – we were constantly play-acting, like children, our own detective story with all its mythic figures of spies and endangered women. I think, or I hope to think, that it was very necessary we had each other. He needed me because whatever one could think of, as long as it was cinematic and imaginary, or even better, uncanny, I would go along with it with downright exhilaration. I needed him because he let me indulge in the expression of everything I loved, film noir, Godard, Anna Karina, Anna Karenina, he let me be free there, which no one else had ever done, better yet, he rexpected my prattling as if it were gold. There was something else there about me that I had never acknowledged and didn't acknowledge until much later – my anger. Peter's film is all about anger, frustration over something that is dimming us down, shutting us up, and suffocating us by withdrawing our means of expression. I think Peter instinctively knew that this is what was being done to me, even before I knew it. At the time I was going through – laughable as it sounds, it was a serious matter that cost me two years – a lot of bureaucratic trouble with the Austrian school system, something I considered so beneath me that I was on the constant brink of a breakdown. What nobody knew was that simmering beneath my dreamy-child façade was this terrible aggression over the system. I still have that aggression, but the film let me play it out. I got to be a terrorist. I didn't even know how badly I had wanted to be a terrorist. I had been ignored. I had been put down. I was stuck where I certainly didn't belong. I was being drained of blood. And this, I think, must have been an attribute to the Marias, only it was so obvious that I didn't even need to be aware of it. But that's why I think I worked for him – because I was discouraged, aggressive, unhappy, but, just to stay alive, I still had a way of seeing what might or might not have been there, and I could do that with great enthusiasm.

Our working method was this, which I then assumed to be and now know was rather Godardian (and therefore legitimate): Peter and I would get together in a café. He would tell me, briefly, what I had to say and which emotions should surface (surprise, anger, fear, etc) and then he would improvise. Often, he would provoke me by touching a subject that would embarrass or anger me. I remember once I got so angry I stopped talking to him. Other times, he would ask me to come work at moments that were completely impossible – and I would come anyway, and be tired, half-sick, or drunk, or bored, or upset over something, and it all would go into the character. So I never really got to act at all, unless during certain conversations. And then sometimes we would just let go and hop about and it was terrible, terrible fun because I got to be angry, and I got to be myself, which was something the rest of the world wasn't letting me be. It's obviously ironic that this had to happen when I wasn't being myself, but one of the Marias.

Re: sophie
Thursday, July 8, 2010 8:48 PM
From: "john sorensen"
To: "Peter Whitehead"

p,

sophie is an amazing human being: rare and alive. thank you for sharing this first draft of her document with me. i look forward to the next version with eagerness and joy.

as well, i hope soon to read your head (and the replies that are hatching within it).

also, i have a question re: the 'chaotic fragments': how can you 'suffer' with me when i am working only in ecstasy?

peace,
j

avoiding the end
Friday, July 9, 2010 6:31 PM
From: "Peter Whitehead"
To: "john sorensen"

VOID in the end... a domain where you fear to trespass?

too close to the bone? herewith the article I wrote in the last month...

peter

END shot...
12 may 2010

Fellini! It seemed clear. But then the doubts. Was it "La Dolce Vita" or "Fellini 8½?" The VHS tapes lost in attic. And so much also lost in the attic of my mind. But then a flash, not a flash-back but a flash-forward. Might this forgetting perhaps show the continuity of Fellini's films? He, like all great directors, suffering the unconscious controlling "monster" that dictates the gyres of the every narrative; denoted by the similarity of end shots, always arriving at the same end point, that ties up all the loose Ends?

Or L'Avventura? The end is a void. Absence. Is She dead or has She abandoned him? Is this why Antonioni made films? Fear of the End Shot? In life? The Pavese novel, "Le Amiche": The Girlfriends. Is it film as well as woman which embodies betrayal... Antonioni's fear that the End in life and film, is inevitably the same. Suddenly, She is no longer there.

For Fellini or Antonioni, is the act of making a film inextricably linked at that deep level to the act of "making" HER? Woman. Dancing Girl. Clown. The End of "BLOW UP", the circus of clowns, people lucky enough to be able to fool about and be, simply, happy. All his films end with a return of the Circle. The Cycle. The Circus.

The end shot of every Bergman film that I saw and re-saw and saw-again, endlessly returning, not prepared to accept there had been an Ending. Closure. An End would mean there is no God. Only a void. I'd return again and again, seeking to deny the End Shot, decimated and lonely, passing the couple in the back row, unaware the End Shot had passed, locked in the eternity of a tense present tense, in an (inner) embrace without ending. In the films, the lovely young blonde girls who promise to stay with you forever. My loving them all, and also the Inevitable Betrayers, as in The Silence, Persona, the older woman, the actress, having come full stop with words. Beyond the End Line she had spoken: Silence. Electra. The older women that Bergman feared, strong enough to disappear, never to be possessed. Forever.

All the End Shots, the final title: BOLD WHITE letters on a BLACK SCREEN. "SLUT". An unseemly, inadvertent comment on those females, fighting with their demons. God, guilt, sex, men: traumas for which there is never an End.

Perhaps my self-portrait, Pierrot le Fou, blue-faced Belmondo becoming a puff of smoke on the cliff top. No; Fellini! The party goers, after the strip tease, the husband's return to see his wife naked on the floor, caressing herself... then the long meandering End Shot, drunken guests stroll onto the beach... where, staring at them, with its hideous eye, the huge ugly monster, such a monster as swims in the personal oceanic unconscious of us all. Was it "La Dolce Vita"? I am not sure.

I prefer the uncertainty of Antonioni. In which there can be no end: no end shot... no closure. It is only Reason and rationality that ends with an End Dot.

Peter Whitehead.

stops & starts
Saturday, July 10, 2010 12:58 PM
From: "john sorensen"
To: 'Peter Whitehead"

p,

thank you for this end without end (amen).
you make me want to continue beginning.

peace,
j

Re: NYTimes.com: Robert F. Boyle, Film Designer for Hitchcock, Dies at 100
Saturday, August 14, 2010 9:12 AM
From: "Peter Whitehead"
To: "john sorensen"

dear John

I am SO SO sorry not to have been in touch recently. Many many reasons. I am sure you understand.

The final convulsions of the Framework project have dragged me in and in and down and down… a recent WEEK with Paul here – work round the clock – James Riley also here for 3 days and the 3 of us talking talking – which I hate at the best of times...

...and endless ensuing (forever) problems with distraught sisters of my lost daughter...

...difficult times.

But one day I hope to write more, to say a huge thank-you for all the work and love you put into your project with and for my film! It will go down in history! Talking of which... I am planning to publish a modest "Screenplay – Dossier" – of the film – images, texts, emails, notebooks etc... 120 pages maybe... like the old Lorrimer books... and we will talk in more detail, once that is happening, about doctoring your text towards this new – and everlasting (insh'Allah)... context. Daunting and haunting... are not the only words!

very very best wishes

shantih shantih shantih

peter.

PS Paul has a pot for you! I felt there was something soft and subtle and Zen about it. I hope you like it!

hello-ing

Saturday, August 14, 2010 6:22 PM
From: "john sorensen"
To: "Peter Whitehead"

Dear Peter,

Thank you for your kind message – it's always a joy for me to hear from you.

I'm sorry for the pain and sorrows that continue for you and your family after the terrible loss of daughter and sister. You are all very much in my thoughts and meditations, and I hope that healing will come... as best as is possible.

It sounds as if the 'Framework' work has been both exhausting and productive, and I'm eager to see how it all turns out. I hope that you will be pleased by the final version of our own 'e-ncounter' text. I feel that there is something beautiful and rare about it, and I'm curious to hear how people respond to it.

I like the idea of the 'Screenplay-Dossier' book for TF, and hope to hear more about this project soon. Please let me know if there is anything I may do to help with it.

Finally, I offer thanks beyond thanks for your generous en-route gift of the 'soft and subtle and Zen' pot. It is already precious to me, and I am grateful for your kindness in this and in all things.

May Peace and Peace and Peace (still) be everywhere.

Love,
j

the mystical filmmaker

Thursday, August 19, 2010 10:37 AM
From: "john sorensen"
To: "Peter Whitehead"

p,

yesterday i read an essay about 'the mystical artist,' and i came across an interesting paragraph, which struck me as having an important application to cinema. while i was reading it, my mind automatically changed to the word 'artist' to 'filmmaker' and i saw it this way:

'In his suggestive and allusive language, the mystical filmmaker often approaches the methods of music. When he does this, his statements do not give information. They operate a kind of enchantment which dilates the consciousness of the audience to a point at which it is able to apprehend new aspects of the world.'

...in a way, this is what i am hoping to achieve in the film that i am preparing with the sudanese. as well, it is a useful description of how i experienced your new film.

peace,
j

Re: the mystical filmmaker
Thursday, August 19, 2010 11:05 AM
From: "Peter Whitehead"
To: "john sorensen"

j

Thank you for this. Makes a lot clear. My TER film is still a mystery to me... where the hell did it come from?

Best wishes for your new film... I hope I will see it one day.

peter

www.ingramcontent.com/pod-product-compliance
Lightning Source LLC
Chambersburg PA
CBHW061031100726
47911CB00006B/154

* 9 7 8 0 9 9 0 5 3 0 8 5 5 *